Short Studies in Private International Law

Short Studies in Private International Law are short-book publications devoted to topics in private international law, in particular international and European civil procedure. The volumes can be a result of papers presented at conferences but can also consist of short monographs or edited volumes on private international law, aimed to inform academics and practitioners timely of recent developments. The hardcover books are compact volumes of 100–150 pages and are characterized by fast, global electronic dissemination, standard publishing contracts, standardized manuscript preparation and formatting guidelines, and expedited production schedules.

More information about this series at http://www.springer.com/series/15450

Vesna Lazić · Steven Stuij
Editors

International Dispute Resolution

Selected Issues in International Litigation and Arbitration

Guest Editor: Ton Jongbloed

ASSER PRESS

Springer

Editors
Vesna Lazić
Private International Law
T.M.C. Asser Instituut
The Hague
The Netherlands

Steven Stuij
Erasmus School of Law
Rotterdam
The Netherlands

ISSN 2522-8145 ISSN 2522-8153 (electronic)
Short Studies in Private International Law
ISBN 978-94-6265-251-4 ISBN 978-94-6265-252-1 (eBook)
https://doi.org/10.1007/978-94-6265-252-1

Library of Congress Control Number: 2018942004

Published by T.M.C. ASSER PRESS, The Hague, The Netherlands www.asserpress.nl
Produced and distributed for T.M.C. ASSER PRESS by Springer-Verlag Berlin Heidelberg

Printed on acid-free paper

This T.M.C. ASSER PRESS imprint is published by the registered company Springer-Verlag GmbH, DE part of Springer Nature
The registered company address is: Heidelberger Platz 3, 14197 Berlin, Germany

Contents

Chapter 1
Considerations on the Impact of EU Law on National Civil Procedure: Recent Examples from Belgium

Janek Tomasz Nowak

Contents

This contribution is based on a presentation given at the 21st Ius Commune congress in Maastricht, the Netherlands, on 24–25 November 2016. The text was finalised on 12 July 2017. Subsequent evolutions have not been taken into account, apart from the amendment to Article 806 Belgian Judicial Code and the Conclusions of Advocate-General Sharpston in *Karel de Grote* (C-147/16). Important developments in 2018 have been added as a footnote without further analysis. I would like to thank Professor V. Lazic and Mr. S. Stuij for their helpful comments on the draft version, which have improved the text considerably. I am equally indebted to Dr. S. Sobrie. I would also like to thank Professor T. Jongbloed for the opportunity to present at the workshop and to contribute to this volume. All mistakes remain my own.

J. T. Nowak (✉)
Max Planck Institute for Procedural Law, Luxembourg, Luxembourg
e-mail: janek.nowak@mpi.lu

J. T. Nowak
MCI Management School, Innsbruck, Austria

J. T. Nowak
Institute for European Law, KU Leuven, Belgium

V. Lazić and S. Stuij (eds.), *International Dispute Resolution*,
Short Studies in Private International Law,
https://doi.org/10.1007/978-94-6265-252-1_1

Abstract While the impact of EU law on national civil procedure is strongly visible in cross-border proceedings, it has potentially a much stronger effect in internal proceedings. Yet its visibility in regard of a domestic context is until today limited, both in practice and in research. This contribution attempts to shed light on the impact of EU law on internal national civil procedure by providing for a number of brief case studies on Belgian civil procedure. The relevance of EU law for the national debate will be considered, as well as its impact on the regulation of civil procedure. Subsequently, the case studies will be used to provide for a number of general considerations regarding the impact of EU law on national civil procedure. These considerations transcend the Belgian legal order and have as their aim to foster the debate on the future of civil procedure in an EU law context.

Keywords Civil procedure · EU law · Court of Justice of the European Union · Effectiveness · National procedural autonomy · Belgium · *Ex officio* application · Costs for expertise · Private damages for competition law violations · Trade Secrets · Fragmentation of civil procedure · Regulation of civil procedure

1.1 Introduction

A considerable part of substantive law in EU Member States is affected by EU law in one way or another. When a dispute arises involving points of EU law, it is the task of the courts of the Member States to provide for a solution in line with EU law. They are the 'ordinary courts' of EU law,[1] the Court of Justice of the European Union (CJEU) only having reserved jurisdiction for a limited number of matters.[2]

The conduct of litigation before national courts is regulated by national procedural law. This is not different when matters of EU law are involved.[3] National courts thus apply national rules of procedure when deciding cases involving an EU law element. It therefore comes primarily to the Member States to provide for an appropriate procedural law framework. However, procedural law can have an

---

[1] Opinion of 8 March 2011, *Draft agreement on the European and Community Patents Court*, 1/09, EU:C:2011:123, para 80.

[2] Article 256 TFEU in conjunction with Article 51 Protocol (No 3) on the statute of the Court of Justice of the European Union

[3] Kakouris 1997, p. 1394.

impact on the application of substantive law,[4] limiting its effects. In order to overcome difficulties in this regard the Court of Justice (CJ) has laid down an effectiveness doctrine, allowing national courts to disregard national rules of procedure obstructing the effective application of EU substantive law.[5] Also the EU legislator has enacted rules on procedural law with the aim of securing the proper application and enforcement of substantive EU law.[6]

This contribution considers the (potential) impact of EU law on national civil procedure. In the first part I will provide a number of general considerations regarding the relevance of EU law for national civil procedure and the functioning of the effectiveness requirement. In the second part I will give a number of examples of the impact of EU legislation and EU case law on national civil procedure in Belgium. Building on this, I will develop a number of broader insights on the difference in approach to civil procedure at EU and at Member State level. I will use these insights to address in the final part a number of consequences of EU law interference with national civil procedure, highlighting the importance of having a proper debate regarding the impact of EU law on national civil procedure.

1.2 EU Law Requirements for National Civil Procedure: The Overarching Framework

1.2.1 The Concept of National Procedural Autonomy

1.2.1.1 Origins

The system of judicial protection in the European Union is characterised by its decentralised nature.[7] Member States' courts have been entrusted with the task of applying and enforcing EU substantive law in day-to-day situations.[8] They use for this purpose their own national procedural law. The application of national procedural law to disputes involving EU law elements has given rise to a number of questions. It was acknowledged that the unrestricted application of national

[4] Zekoll 2006, p. 1336.

[5] Reich 2014, pp. 89–131; Kulms 2013, pp. 21–22.

[6] See, for example, Directive 2009/22/EC of the European Parliament and of the Council of 23 April 2009 on injunctions for the protection of consumers' interests, *O.J.* 2009, L 110/30, replacing Directive 98/27/EC of the European Parliament and of the Council of 19 May 1998 on injunctions for the protection of consumers' interests, *O.J.* 1998, L 166/51 and Directive 2010/104/EU of the European Parliament and of the Council of 26 November 2014 on certain rules governing actions for damages under national law for infringements of the competition law provisions of the Member States and of the European Union, *O.J.* 2014, L 349/1.

[7] Schermers and Waelbroeck 2001, p. 197.

[8] Opinion of 8 March 2011, *Draft agreement on the European and Community Patents Court*, 1/09, EU:C:2011:123, paras 66–69.

procedural law may have an impact on the effective application of EU substantive law. In response to this concern, the Court of Justice has developed a so-called doctrine of national procedural autonomy.[9] The doctrine entails that in the absence of harmonised rules on the matter, Member States are free to enact rules of national procedural law provided that claims based on EU law are not treated less favourably than similar claims based on national law (principle of equivalence)[10] and that national procedural rules do not make the enforcement of rights deriving from EU law virtually impossible or excessively difficult (principle of effectiveness).[11] This contribution will focus on the effectiveness requirement of the Court's doctrine.

The notion 'national procedural autonomy' is often used in the legal and political debate to refer to the case law of the Court of Justice concerning national procedural law. It should be pointed out, however, that the Court did not coin the term national procedural autonomy. The notion has been derived from the notion of '*autonomie institutionnelle*', used already in 1972 by Rideau as a doctrinal framework to describe the relationship between EU substantive law and Member State law, *inter alia* procedural law.[12] It should be noted that this predates the Court's decisions in *Rewe* and *Comet.* The notion of autonomy was thus not specifically conceived as a description of the case law of the Court of Justice on national procedural law; it was only later on that it was used in legal doctrine to refer to the Court's case law on national procedural rules because it concerned largely a similar issue. It does, however, not accurately describe the Court's case law on the matter and remains highly contested in legal doctrine.[13] This is even so despite the fact that the Court has started referring to the concept of 'national procedural autonomy' in its decisions since in the beginning of the 2000s.[14]

1.2.1.2 The Issue of Autonomy

Member States Are Not Autonomous When Enacting Rules of Civil Procedure

A problematic aspect of the notion 'national procedural autonomy' is the concept of 'autonomy',[15] which puts too much emphasis on the freedom of the Member States

[9] Judgment of 16 December 1976, *Rewe*, 33/76, EU:C:1976:188 and Judgment of 16 December 1976, *Comet*, 45/76, EU:C:1976:191. See also Galetta 2010, pp. 118–119.

[10] König 2011, pp. 92–104.

[11] Kulms 2013, pp. 21–22.

[12] Rideau 1972, p. 884; Haapaniemi 2009, p. 89.

[13] Póltorak 2015, pp. 33–35; Bobek 2012, p. 320–322; Kakouris 1997, p. 1390.

[14] Judgment of 7 January 2004, *Wells*, C-201/02, EU:C:2004:12, para 67. Before, the concept of procedural autonomy was mainly used in the argumentation of the parties or in competition law appeals concerning the actual autonomy of courts in light of Article 6 ECHR. It was, however, not linked to the requirements of equivalence and effectiveness until the Court's judgment in *Wells*.

[15] Bobek 2012, p. 321.

to enact procedural rules[16] and minimalises the ever increasing impact of the effectiveness requirement on national procedural law.[17] A glance at the case law of the Court shows that the concept of 'autonomy' is misguiding in this regard,[18] its decisions touching upon a variety of procedural themes such as time-limits,[19] evidence,[20] standing,[21] competence,[22] jurisdiction,[23] *ex officio* application,[24] availability of remedies[25] and the principle of *res judicata.*[26]

A good example to illustrate this point concerns the Spanish procedural framework for mortgage enforcement proceedings. It appeared that parties being faced with enforcement proceedings could not seek the termination of these proceedings on account that the contractual term on which the right to seek enforcement was based was unfair. Such claim could not be raised in enforcement proceedings but had to be pursued in separate proceedings to obtain a declaratory judgment. These declaratory proceedings did, however, not have a suspensive effect on the actual enforcement proceedings. The Court of Justice held in *Aziz* that such a procedural framework rendered the application of the Unfair Contract Terms Directive (hereafter 'UCTD')[27] excessively difficult in so far as it made it impossible for the court hearing the declaratory proceedings to grant interim relief capable of staying or terminating the mortgage enforcement proceedings, where such relief was necessary to ensure the full effectiveness of its final decision.[28] The Spanish legal framework was subsequently amended, allowing parties to raise the unfairness of contract terms in the context of mortgage enforcement proceedings to resist enforcement.[29] The choice of the Spanish legislator to regulate its mortgage enforcement proceedings in a certain manner was thus invalidated by the Court of Justice on account that it interfered with the effective application of the UCTD.

---

16 Półtorak 2015, p. 37.

17 Bobek 2012, pp. 322–323.

18 Lenaerts et al. 2014, pp. 118–156; Le Baut-Ferrarese 2010, p. 81.

19 Judgment of 8 July 2010, *Bulicke*, C-246/09, EU:C:2010:418, paras 36–37.

20 Judgment of 9 November 1983, *San Giorgio*, 199/82, EU:C:1983:318, para 14.

21 Judgment of 8 March 2011, *Lesoochranárske zoskupenie*, C-240/09, EU:C:2011:125, para 52.

22 Judgment of 15 April 2008, *Impact*, C-268/06, EU:C:2008:223, para 51; Judgment of 27 June 2013, *Agrokonsulting*, C-93/12, EU:C:2013:432, para 37.

23 Order of 12 June 2008, *Vasilakis*, C-364/07, EU:C:2008:346, paras 149–150.

24 Judgment of 14 December 1995, *van Schijndel and van Veen*, C-430/93 and C-431/93, EU:C:1995:441.

25 Order of 14 November 2013, *Banco Popular Español*, C-537/12 and C-116/13, EU:C:2013:759, paras 48–59.

26 Judgment of 3 September 2009, *Fallimento Olimpiclub*, C-2/08, EU:C:2009:506, para 31.

27 Council Directive 93/13/EEC of 5 April 1993 on unfair terms in consumer contracts, *O.J.* 1993, L 95/29.

28 Judgment of 14 March 2013, *Aziz*, C-415/11, EU:C:2013:164, para 63.

29 Law No 1/2013 of 14 May 2013 laying down measures for the strengthening of the protection of mortgagors, the restructuring of debt and social rent (Ley 1/2013 de medidas para reforzar la protección a los deudores hipotecarios, reestructuración de deuda y alquiler social), BOE N° 116 of 15 May 2013, p. 36373.

Similar to other rules of national law, rules of civil procedure can thus be considered as measures by which a Member State ensures the proper application of EU substantive law. If those rules prove to be counterproductive to that aim,[30] they might need to be altered or set aside (negative harmonisation).[31] There exists in this regard no greater freedom for Member States to maintain rules that potentially obstruct the implementation of EU law than in any other area of law. From an EU law perspective, procedural rules are on par with substantive rules or rules of administrative procedure.[32]

The EU Has an Extensive Competence to Enact Rules of Civil Procedure

The emphasis that is being put on the notion of 'autonomy' also negates the first part of the Court's holding in the *Rewe* and *Comet* decisions, as it gives the impression that there is only limited competence for the EU to intervene on matters of procedural law.[33] This is, however, an incorrect view. Currently, an increasing body of procedural rules is being enacted by the EU legislator, further disproving the idea that a special kind of autonomy exists for the Member States in relation to procedural law.[34]

It should be noted that no general competence clause exists for the EU to enact procedural law. However, procedural rules are considered to be rules necessary for the enforcement of EU substantive law[35] and can therefore be adopted on the basis of the competence provision for a specific substantive law area (positive harmonisation). For example, the competence for consumer policy also implies a competence to lay down procedural rules contributing to the application and enforcement of EU consumer law.[36] The EU does not need a procedural competence clause to enact procedural law.

The enactment of a procedural rule by the EU legislator entails the consequence that there is no longer any freedom for the Member States to enact procedural rules

[30] Adinolfi 2012, pp. 299–300.

[31] Normand 2006, p. 381; Van Gerven 2000, pp. 506–509; Kakouris 1997, p. 1396.

[32] Kovar 1973, pp. 201 et seq: "On voit mal les raisons qui pourraient justifier l'octroi d'une immunité particulière aux règles du droit judiciaire."

[33] Kakouris 1997, pp. 1396–1397.

[34] Wilman 2015, pp. 404–405; Le Baut-Ferrarese 2010, p. 81. See also a recent resolution of the European Parliament, calling the European Commission to launch a proposal for the minimum harmonisation of civil procedure in the Member States: European Parliament resolution of 4 July 2017 with recommendations to the Commission on common minimum standards of civil procedure in the European Union, P8_TA(2017)0282.

[35] Adinolfi 2012, p. 303.

[36] See in this regard the Injunctions Directive, which was based on the EU's internal market competence. That competence was mainly used to adopt substantive consumer law provisions. Also note that the recitals of the Directive make a connection between the adoption of the Directive and the need to secure the effective enforcement of a numbers of substantive consumer law Directives.

on similar matters. This is a logical consequence of the principle of primacy and the pre-emption principle.[37] Member States cannot deviate from EU rules and the same goes when those rules are of a procedural nature. An example can be found in the Injunctions Directive, which obliges Member States to create an injunction procedure that allows for the cessation or prohibition of any infringement of a number of consumer law directives.[38] Member States cannot do anything else but comply with this obligation. The fact that a Member State is of the opinion that other procedural instruments are more appropriate for that purpose is irrelevant; the EU legislator has made the determination that an injunction is an appropriate instrument and Member States have to adhere to this choice. A strict primacy test applies in this regard, discarding any national rules that deviate from the EU standard. The assessment of the Court of Justice will in such a situation not entail an evaluation of the appropriateness of the choices made by the national legislator, but merely a verification of the correct implementation of the relevant EU rules.

An in-between position can be found in relation to EU directives giving Member States some latitude in implementing procedural provisions. This is for example the case for Article 14 IP Enforcement Directive,[39] which provides that:

> Member States shall ensure that reasonable and proportionate legal costs and other expenses incurred by the successful party shall, as a general rule, be borne by the unsuccessful party, unless equity does not allow this.

While Member States retain a margin of discretion when it comes to determining what reasonable and proportionate costs entail, the Court of Justice will evaluate national implementing measures in the light of the goals of the specific directive, providing for a close scrutiny of the procedural choices made by the national legislator.[40] This is, however, not a question of 'national procedural autonomy'[41] but of the *effet utile* of the directive.[42]

---

[37] Article 2(2) TFEU.

[38] Directive 2009/22/EC of the European Parliament and of the Council of 23 April 2009 on injunctions for the protection of consumers' interests, *O.J.* 2009, L 110/30, replacing Directive 98/27/EC of the European Parliament and of the Council of 19 May 1998 on injunctions for the protection of consumers' interests, *O.J.* 1998, L 166/51.

[39] Directive 2004/48/EC of the European Parliament and of the Council of 29 April 2004 on the enforcement of intellectual property rights, O.J. 2004, L 157/45 and Corrigendum, *O.J.* 2004, L 195/16. (Hereafter 'IP Enforcement Directive' or 'IPED').

[40] Hess 2010, p. 627. Note that also in such cases Article 47 CFR may be part of the analysis. A rule that allows for the effective enforcement of EU law does not necessarily correspond to the right to effective judicial protection.

[41] Wilman 2015, p. 409.

[42] Judgment of 5 April 2017, *Marina del Mediterráneo*, C-391/15, EU:C:2017:268, para 33; Judgment of 17 July 2014, *Sánchez Morcillo*, C-169/14, EU:C:2014:2009, para 50.

1.2.1.3 The Relevance of Fundamental Rights

I should also briefly mention a third EU law constraint on national procedural law, namely the Charter of Fundamental Rights (hereafter 'Charter' or 'CFR'). Article 47 CFR lays down the right to an effective remedy before a court. According to Article 51 CFR and the explanations accompanying Article 47 CFR,[43] Member States are bound by the Charter when acting in the scope of EU law. This means that the standard of Article 47 CFR applies each time national civil procedure is being used to apply and enforce EU law obligations. It may even require Member States to go beyond the standard laid down in Articles 6 and 13 ECHR, the CFR providing for a higher level of judicial protection.[44]

Further to this, it should be pointed out that the fundamental rights standard applies regardless of the existence of specific procedural rules laid down at EU level. National civil procedure is thus not only subject to a general effectiveness test that verifies whether national procedural law allows for the effective application of EU substantive law but also to a strict fundamental rights test that verifies whether national procedural law guarantees an effective remedy. Even in the absence of EU rules on procedural law, Member States are constrained by EU law in a double way regarding their freedom to enact rules of civil procedure.

Adding to this, it should be noted that the effective application of EU law itself can be limited by the right to a fair trial as laid down in Article 47 CFR.[45] After all, the fundamental right to effective judicial protection is a minimum standard to which also the Court and the EU legislator must adhere, unless it appears to be justifiable to deviate from that standard. The effective application of EU substantive law is thus not absolute.

Lastly, while Article 47 CFR is part of the general framework of the impact of EU law on national civil procedure, I will not specifically deal with its impact in the remainder of this contribution. This is a deliberate choice, which reflects the aim of this contribution, namely to uncover the specific impact of EU law effectiveness requirements on national civil procedure. The impact of the application of the principle of effective judicial protection is, however, not specific to the EU as the principle also exists in relation to the European Convention of Human Rights and the Strasbourg case law, which generates similar effects. For that reason, it has been left out of the following analysis.

---

[43] Explanations relating to the Charter of Fundamental Rights (2007/C 303/02), *O.J.* 2007, C 303/17.

[44] Judgment of 22 December 2010, *DEB*, C-279/09, EU:C:2010:811, para 35.

[45] Judgment of 21 February 2013, *Banif Plus Bank*, C-472/11, EU:C:2013:88, para 29.

1.2.2 *EU Law as a Multiple Constraint on National Civil Procedure*

EU law requirements for national civil procedure may originate in multiple sources: an obligation laid down in an EU instrument (*primacy/effet utile*), the effective application of EU substantive law (*principle of effectiveness*), or the Charter of Fundamental Rights of the European Union (*principle of effective judicial protection*). When national civil procedure comes within the scope of EU law, the freedom on part of the national legislator to enact procedural rules is thus severely limited. The concept of 'national procedural autonomy' is therefore not an accurate reflection of the actual situation. The continued use of it is, however, problematic as it obfuscates the debate on the impact of EU law on national procedural law, especially in regard of civil procedure.

1.3 Civil Procedure in EU Legislation and EU Case Law: Recent Examples and Impact on the Belgian Legal Order

In this section I will illustrate the impact of the effectiveness requirement by providing some recent examples from Belgium. I will focus on the effects of EU legislation providing for procedural rules as well as the Court's case law concerning the interplay of national rules of civil procedure and the effective application of EU substantive law. For reasons mentioned above, I will not include the specific impact of the EU principle of effective judicial protection on national civil procedure.

In the first subsection, I will focus on the impact of the Court's case law on Belgian national civil procedure. The second subsection addresses a number of recent legislative initiatives taken at EU level and how they impact on the Belgian legal order. The twofold approach reflects the two sources from which EU law influence over national civil procedure is stemming, namely the EU judiciary and the EU legislator.

1.3.1 *National Civil Procedure in the Case Law of the Court of Justice*

1.3.1.1 Introduction

This subsection illustrates how the Court of Justice uses the effectiveness requirement as a means to assess the appropriateness of national procedural law in light of EU substantive law (Sect. 1.3.1.2) and to evaluate the implementation of EU procedural legislation in national law (Sect. 1.3.1.3). It also looks at the ramifications of the case law in the Belgian legal order and the relevance of the Court's decisions for broader debates in Belgian civil procedure.

1.3.1.2 *Ex Officio* Application of the Unfair Contract Terms Directive

General

The case law of the Court of Justice on the *ex officio* application of EU law is embedded in the traditional doctrine of 'national procedural autonomy', as exemplified by the Court's decision in *van Schijndel and van Veen*.[46] In matters concerning consumer protection, its approach is however slightly different. In the context of the Unfair Contract Terms Directive, a line of case law has developed that obliges national courts to raise the unfairness of contractual terms in consumer contracts both within the framework of the national procedural autonomy doctrine (*principle of effectiveness*) and the application of the UCTD (*primacy/effet utile*).[47] This line of case law was cautiously expanded to a number of other consumer law directives later on.[48] It remains, however, unclear to which extent the decisions in relation to the UCTD are unreservedly applicable in other contexts. I will therefore concentrate on the *ex officio* application of the UCTD, where the development is the strongest.

Article 6 UCTD provides that unfair contract terms should not be binding upon consumers. The Court of Justice inferred from this a duty for national courts to raise and apply the UCTD of their own motion. This implies three main tasks: (1) verifying whether a contract term comes within the scope of the UCTD, if necessary by taking measures of inquiry *ex officio*;[49] (2) raising and applying the UCTD *ex officio*, meaning evaluating whether an imbalance exists between the contracting parties and whether the principle of good faith has been compromised;[50] (3) making sure that the unfair contract term does not bind the consumer,[51] which in many legal systems means that the unfair contract term should be declared void. While exercising these tasks they should respect the right to a fair trial[52] and leave the consumer the possibility to denounce the protection conferred upon it by the UCTD after a debate on the matter.[53] One may thus wonder whether it is really a matter of *ex officio* application or rather a duty to inform the consumer.

---

[46] Judgment of 14 December 1995, *van Schijndel and van Veen*, C-430/93 and C-431/93, EU:C:1995:441.

[47] Lenaerts et al. 2014, pp. 135–136.

[48] Judgment of 4 October 2007, *Rampion*, C-429/05, EU:C:2007:575; Judgment of 17 December 2009, *Martín Martín*, C-227/08, EU:C:2009:792.

[49] Judgment of 9 November 2010, *VB Pénzügyi Lízing*, C-137/08, EU:C:2010:659, para 56.

[50] Judgment of 4 June 2009, *Pannon*, C-243/08, EU:C:2009:350, para 32.

[51] Judgment of 30 May 2013, *Asbeek Brusse*, C-488/11, EU:C:2013:341, para 49.

[52] *Banif Plus Bank*, para 31.

[53] *Pannon*, para 33.

Interestingly, Article 6 UCTD does not make any reference to *ex officio* application by judges. The Court has nevertheless read into this provision a duty of *ex officio* application by taking into account the specifics of consumer litigation. The Court's rationale is based on the assumption that the amounts involved in consumer disputes are often limited and disproportionately low in relation to lawyers' fees, which may deter consumers from seeking representation in order to contest a claim based on an unfair contract term. A consumer may then default, especially in the case of unfair forum clauses.[54] In case the consumer would nevertheless appear and represent her or himself, the Court assumes that the consumer is not always properly informed about the rights conferred upon her or him by the UCTD and will not avail her or himself of them properly.[55] If national procedural law would then leave it to the consumer to invoke the UCTD, this would entail the consequence that the UCTD would not be applied and that its effects and long term policy goals would not be realised.[56] Intervention unconnected to the actual parties to the contract may thus be necessary.[57] The Court then determined that such intervention implies the *ex officio* application of the UCTD by the national judge.[58] National judges are thus effectively entrusted with the task of applying and enforcing the UCTD in the Member States.

Note that the obligation to apply the UCTD is directly based on the directive only in case of ordinary first-instance proceedings. In case of special proceedings, such as enforcement proceedings[59] or payment order proceedings,[60] the Court has analysed the lack of a duty for the judge to apply the UCTD *ex officio* through the lens of the national procedural autonomy doctrine and did not base such obligation directly on the UCTD. Why it did so is not entirely clear. Perhaps the Court signals that a general obligation to apply the UCTD *ex officio* does not exist in special proceedings and that the obligation to apply the UCTD *ex officio* in those cases was a solution tailored to a specific problem that existed in a particular Member State. That being said, the outcomes of *Pannon* and *Banco Español de Crédito* are nevertheless the same, regardless of the route taken by the Court; a duty of *ex officio* application exists. At times the principle of effectiveness allows for as little leeway as the primacy/*effet utile* approach.

Next to the need for the effective application of the UCTD, the Court also pointed at the importance of the UCTD from a policy perspective, classifying it as a rule on par with national rules of public policy.[61] It did so because many Member

[54] Judgment of 27 June 2000, *Océano Grupo Editorial*, C-240/98 to C-244/98, EU:C:2000:346, para 26.

[55] Ibid.

[56] Ibid.

[57] *Océano Grupo Editorial*, para 27.

[58] *Océano Grupo Editorial*, para 29.

[59] *Aziz*, para 49.

[60] *Banco Español de Crédito*, para 45.

[61] Judgment of 6 October 2009, *Asturcom*, C-40/08, EU:C:2009:615, paras 51–52.

States know a concept of public policy in relation to a duty of *ex officio* application. By taking this approach, the Court was able to reconcile the need for an effective application of the UCTD with existing rules of national civil procedure. The problem is that in various Member States consumer law as such is not considered to be of public policy and that the nullity of contract terms—closely linked to the idea of the UCTD—is equally not always a matter of public policy.[62] Where a Member State bases the *ex officio* application of the law on the presence of an issue of public policy, a strict application of that requirement may lead to the UCTD not being applied *ex officio* by judges. The issue became problematic in Belgium after the 2015 reform of default proceedings, requiring courts to verify only matters of public policy in the context of default proceedings.

The 2015 Reform of Default Proceedings in Belgium

In 2015 the Belgian Judicial Code (hereafter 'JC')[63] was amended on various points as part of a series of reforms to modernise civil procedure.[64] One of these points concerned Article 806 JC on default proceedings. The aim of the amendment was to settle a longstanding discussion within the Belgian legal order, namely the task of the judge in default proceedings.[65] One part of the judiciary considered it to be its task to apply the law *ex officio* and to maximise protection for the defaulting party; another part of the judiciary considered itself restrained and was only prepared to invoke rules of a public policy nature.[66] The 2015 amendments codified the minimalist approach, courts only being required to apply rules of a public policy nature in default proceedings.[67]

The amendment has led to a debate in the Belgian legal order about the extent to which judges were restrained by Article 806 JC in applying the law *ex officio*.[68] It should be pointed out in this regard that consumer law as such is not considered to be part of the rules of public policy in the Belgian legal order, apart from a number of specific provisions.[69] The laws regarding unfair contract terms are not part of those specific provisions, the Belgian Supreme Court having explicitly ruled so.[70] Conversely, however, the rules of the Civil Code regarding disproportionate penalty

[62] The issue has given rise to the judgment of the Court in *Rampion*. See *Rampion*, para 58.

[63] The code containing the Belgian rules on civil procedure is called 'Gerechtelijk Wetboek'/'Code judiciaire'. I will use the literal English translation throughout this contribution in order to stay as close as possible to its actual name instead of using a functional translation, such as 'Code of Civil Procedure'.

[64] For an overview of the most important changes, see Van Drooghenbroeck 2016a.

[65] Van Drooghenbroeck 2016b, pp. 197–199.

[66] Van Drooghenbroeck 2016b, pp. 199–202.

[67] Van Drooghenbroeck 2016b, p. 203.

[68] Van Drooghenbroeck 2016b, pp. 212–217.

[69] Steennot 2016, p. 430.

[70] Belgian Supreme Court 26 May 2005, Journal des Tribunaux 2005, 679.

and interests clauses are considered to be rules of public policy.[71] Does this mean that there is no problem? Not exactly. While disproportionate penalty and interest clauses are the most common examples of unfair contract terms, the rules regarding unfair contract terms cover a much broader spectrum of potentially unfair contract clauses. Moreover, case law has been reported in which judges have even refused to make use of their general powers to limit *ex officio* disproportionate penalty and interest clauses following the amendment of Article 806 JC.[72] The 2015 amendment has therefore raised questions within the judiciary and legal doctrine regarding the application of the rules on unfair contract terms in default proceedings.[73]

The legislator has responded to these concerns by amending Article 806 JC in the summer of 2017,[74] adding that a judge could also apply of his own motion rules of which a law has stated that a judge could apply them *ex officio*. One could wonder whether this will solve the issue, especially when it comes to unfair contract terms.[75] A solution may be found, however, in the Court's case law on the *ex officio* application of the UCTD. Two approaches can be taken in this regard.

First, one could employ the effectiveness approach. The effective application of the UCTD requires a judge to raise the unfairness of contract terms of its own motion in consumer disputes. National law cannot limit that obligation on account of the principle of primacy of EU law or the principle of effectiveness. If judges would feel that Article 806 JC limits them in this regard, they can merely disregard this limitation. The question is whether this approach is possible in a conflict between two private parties, given the limitations on the horizontal direct effect of EU directives.[76] One could however argue that it is not an issue of direct effect, i.e. creating rights/obligations directly on the basis of the directive, but merely one of primacy, i.e. ousting the conflicting national rule. Also, it creates merely a rule for the judge, not for the parties as such. Since a judge has an obligation to apply EU law correctly,[77] he or she will be required to oust the conflicting national rule that limits his power to raise the UCTD *ex officio*. That in itself would not create any obligations on the part of a private individual but merely entail adverse

[71] Van Orshoven 2016, p. 154.

[72] Justice of the Peace Genk, 15 December 2015, Revue de Droit Judiciaire et de la Preuve 2016, 228.

[73] Steennot 2017, p. 123. These concerns were, however, not unequivocally shared by legal doctrine. See Mosselmans 2016–2017, p. 23 and Van Orshoven 2016, p. 154.

[74] Article 138 Law on the simplification, harmonisation, informatisation and modernisation of provisions of civil law and civil procedural law as well as regarding the profession of the notary, and regarding various provisions concerning the justice system (Loi portant simplification, harmonisation, informatisation et modernisation de dispositions de droit civil et de procédure civile ainsi que du notariat, et portant diverses mesures en matière de justice), *Belgian State Gazette* 24 July 2017, 75168.

[75] Steennot 2017, p. 123; Scheers and Thiriar 2017–2018, p. 723.

[76] Judgment of 14 July 1994, *Faccini Dori*, C-91/92, EU:C:1994:292, paras 19–26.

[77] Judgment of 26 October 2016, *Canal Digital Danmark*, C-611/14, EU:C:2016:800, paras 30–32.

consequences resulting from the fact that the national court is now obliged to apply the UCTD *ex officio*. This is allowed according to the case law of the Court of Justice;[78] no rights or obligations are being created for individuals.[79]

It would also be possible to circumvent the direct effect issue altogether. Therefore, we turn to the other part of the 'national procedural autonomy' doctrine, namely the principle of equivalence. In accordance with that principle, claims based on EU law should not be treated less favourably than claims based on national law.[80] The Court has applied the principle of equivalence a number of times in the context of the *ex officio* application of the UCTD, holding that if national law allows for rules of public policy to be applied *ex officio*, the UCTD should be considered as a rule of public policy for that purpose.[81] The advantage of this approach is that it does not call for a disruption of national procedural rules and that it reconciles the requirements flowing from EU law with the policy choices of the national legislator. It also prevents judges from having to enter into debate on the direct effect of the UCTD in horizontal situations. It requires, however, that judges consider the UCTD and its implementing rules as rules of a public policy nature. This may be problematic because the Belgian Supreme Court has explicitly stated that laws regarding unfair contract terms are as such not of public policy.[82] The question is thus whether judges in all circumstances will make the subtle distinction between 'is a rule of public policy' and 'should be treated as similar to rules of public policy'.[83]

Practice will demonstrate which approach will be taken to overcome the limiting effect of Article 806 JC. Decisions have been reported in which courts have explicitly disregarded Article 806 JC by holding that EU law requires the UCTD and its implementing legislation to be applied *ex officio*.[84] While this is the correct approach, it confirms the argument that Article 806 JC is problematic from an EU law point of view and that the legal framework is currently unclear. The Belgian Supreme Court has already made way for a more extensive interpretation of Article 806 JC, holding that it is for the courts to interpret the scope of Article 806 JC.[85]

---

[78] See in a different situation: Judgment of 7 January 2004, *Wells*, C-201/02, EU:C:2004:14, para 57.

[79] See in this regard Judgment of 26 September 2000, *Unilever Italia*, C-443/98, EU:C:2000:496, para 51.

[80] Judgment of 21 December 2016, *TDC*, C-327/15, EU:C:2016:974, para 92.

[81] Judgment of 6 October 2009, *Asturcom*, C-40/08, EU:C:2009:615, para 52.

[82] See *supra*, note 70.

[83] Steennot 2017, p. 123.

[84] Court of First Instance West-Flanders, 13 September 2016, Rechtskundig Weekblad 2016–2017, 996; Justice of the Peace Bruges, 26 February 2016, Journal des Juges de Paix 2017, 58; Justice of the Peace Westerlo, 2 March 2016, Rechtskundig Weekblad 2016–2017, 273; Justice of the Peace Fléron, 22 March 2016, Journal des Juges de Paix 2016, 272; Justice of the Peace Liège, 11 May 2016, Journal des Juges de Paix 2017, 36.

[85] Belgian Supreme Court 13 December 2016, N° P.16.0412.N; for a comment, see Mosselmans et al. 2016–2017.

This would allow judges to be more flexible. Nevertheless, it will probably take a judgment of the Court of Justice to provide a definite solution to the problem. A reference for a preliminary ruling on the matter is currently pending before it.[86] In her Opinion of 30 November 2017, Advocate-General Sharpston has argued, largely basing herself on the principle of equivalence, that "under Article 806 Judicial Code the national court is obliged to assess of its own motion whether a clause is unfair in the light of Directive 93/13 in the same way as it does for national rules of public policy".[87] In light of its judgment in *Asturcom*,[88] it is very likely that the Court will come to the same conclusion.[89]

1.3.1.3 Rules on the Reimbursement of Party-Appointed Expert Fees and the IP Enforcement Directive

Costs for legal assistance by a lawyer or a party-appointed expert were not recoverable under Belgian law until recently. The Judicial Code of 1967 had explicitly excluded costs for legal assistance from the types of reimbursable costs.[90] In 2004 the Belgian Supreme Court accepted the principle that costs for legal assistance could form part of the damage in a contractual liability claim, provided that such costs were necessary to bring the case.[91] Later on, this case law was extended to non-contractual liability claims.[92]

The application of a fault liability regime to the reimbursement of costs for legal assistance was not without problems. First, the regime could only find application when a claim concerned an issue of fault liability.[93] Other areas were thus excluded from the possibility to recover fees for legal assistance, for example litigation in fiscal, social or family matters. Second, the application of a fault liability regime created a problem of procedural equality between the parties to the proceedings. An applicant party claiming damages could have the costs for legal assistance reimbursed by including these as part of the damage. A defendant party, however, did not incur any damage as such and therefore had no basis to seek reimbursement of costs incurred for legal assistance in case his defence would be successful.

---

[86] Request for a preliminary ruling from the Justice of the Peace of Antwerp (Belgium) lodged on 14 March 2016, *Karel de Grote*, C-147/16, *O.J.* 2016, C 211/28, pending.

[87] Opinion of Advocate General Sharpston of 30 November 2017, *Karel de Grote*, C-147/16, EU:C:2017:928, point 36.

[88] See *supra*, note 61.

[89] In a decision of 17 May 2018, the Court of Justice decided that the Belgian judge is obliged to apply the UCTD in default proceedings on the basis of the principle of equivalence. See Judgment of 17 May 2018, *Karel de Grote*, C-147/16,EU:C:2018:320.

[90] De Temmerman 2003, pp. 1015–1023.

[91] Belgian Supreme Court 2 September 2004, Journal des Tribunaux 2004, 684.

[92] Belgian Supreme Court 16 November 2006, Journal des Tribunaux 2007, 14.

[93] Tack 2005, pp. 1302–1303.

Reimbursement of costs for legal assistance was only possible when he could prove that the initiation of legal proceedings by the applicant party constituted a fault in itself. Such requirement made it extremely difficult for a prevailing defendant to recover costs for legal assistance and created an imbalance in judicial proceedings between an applicant and a defendant, contrary to the principle of the equality of arms.[94] Third, the necessity criterion was subject to various interpretations of lower courts, creating uncertainty regarding the types of costs for legal assistance that could be claimed for and to which extent.[95] In 2007, a Law and a Royal Decree were adopted to regulate the recoverability of fees for legal representation.[96] The regime for party-appointed experts remained, however, subject to a fault liability regime.[97]

The issue came to the Court of Justice in the context of a dispute concerning the taxation of costs in patent litigation.[98] United Video Properties (UVP) had filed for an injunction against Telenet to cease all direct and indirect infringements of its European patent for providing storage of data on servers in an on-demand media delivery system.[99] The president of the Antwerp Commercial Court dismissed the claim, holding that UVP's patent failed to meet the condition of novelty. It also admitted Telenet's counterclaim to invalidate the Belgian part of the European Patent.[100] UVP appealed the decision before the Antwerp Court of Appeal. At the same time, proceedings were pending between UVP and Virgin media in the UK courts concerning the same patent. When the London High Court of Justice also ruled that UVP's patent failed to meet the requirement of novelty, UVP discontinued its appeal before the Antwerp Court of Appeal.[101] Telenet asked the Court of Appeal to order UVP to reimburse costs for legal assistance and claimed *inter alia* 44.400 EUR for special technical assistance in the field of patents.[102]

It should be pointed out that Telenet was the defendant in the case. This meant that it had to prove that UVP had made a fault in bringing proceedings against it, which proved to be a high threshold. Telenet considered this requirement to be contrary to Article 14 IPED,[103] which provides that

---

[94] Belgian Constitutional Court of 19 April 2006, N° 57/2006, B.5.1 (available from http://www.const-court.be/public/n/2006/2006-057n.pdf).

[95] Tack 2005, pp. 1307–1308.

[96] Law of 21 April 2007 on the recovery of honorary fees and costs connected to assistance by a lawyer (Loi relative à la répétibilité des honoraires et des frais d'avocat), *Belgian State Gazette* 31 May 2007, 29541; Royal Decree of 26 October 2007, *Belgian State Gazette* 9 November 2007, 56834. For an overview, see van Drooghenbroeck and De Coninck 2008.

[97] Van Drooghenbroeck and De Coninck 2008, p. 51.

[98] Judgment of 28 July 2016, *United Video Properties*, C-57/15, EU:C:2016:611.

[99] *United Video Properties*, para 14.

[100] *United Video Properties*, para 15.

[101] *United Video Properties*, para 16.

[102] *United Video Properties*, para 16.

[103] Directive 2004/48/EC of the European Parliament and of the Council of 29 April 2004 on the enforcement of intellectual property rights, *OJ* 2004, L 157/45 (corrigendum *OJ* 2004, L 195/16).

> Member States shall ensure that reasonable and proportionate legal costs and other expenses incurred by the successful party shall, as a general rule, be borne by the unsuccessful party, unless equity does not allow this.

It argued that the IPED did not require fault liability as a precondition for the reimbursement of fees for technical assistance by an expert.[104]

The Court of Justice held that costs of a technical adviser can in principle be considered to be part of the concept of 'other expenses' within the meaning of Article 14 IPED.[105] However, it made a distinction between costs of identification and research incurred for the purposes of detection of potential infringements of IP rights on the one hand and costs necessary for bringing successful judicial proceedings on the other hand. Only the latter can be considered to be part of 'other expenses' within the meaning of Article 14 Directive.[106] The costs for identification and research are typically of a general nature and cannot be considered to be closely and directly linked to judicial proceedings.[107] Such costs may, however, be part of a damages claim in line with Article 13 Directive.[108] Having established which costs are part of the 'other expenses' a successful party can claim reimbursement for, the Court moved on to decide that Article 14 IPED does not include a condition of fault on the part of the unsuccessful party for reimbursement of such costs.[109]

In a judgment of 8 May 2017, the Antwerp Court of Appeal applied the judgment of the Court of Justice in a parallel case between United Video Properties and Telenet.[110] In this case, Telenet claimed *inter alia* reimbursement of 63.804,25 EUR for expert fees. Telenet had raised similar arguments regarding the application of the national legal framework in light of the IPED.

It should be recalled that the reimbursement regime based on fault liability is a judicial construction that can be discarded rather easily. The national law merely prescribes that a party who discontinues the proceedings is obliged to pay for the costs incurred by the other party[111] and that an unsuccessful party will be required to pay the costs.[112] The Judicial Code lists a number of costs to this extent, but not in an exhaustive way.[113] While costs for party-appointed experts are not included in the list of reimbursable costs, it appears that the national legal framework can be interpreted in conformity with the Directive, regardless of the original intent of the legislator. This is also the line of reasoning followed by the Antwerp Court of Appeal. The Court of Appeal stated that the existing legal framework did not object

---

[104] *United Video Properties*, para 18.

[105] *United Video Properties*, para 34.

[106] *United Video Properties*, para 36.

[107] *United Video Properties*, para 35.

[108] *United Video Properties*, para 36.

[109] *United Video Properties*, para 37.

[110] Court of Appeal Antwerp, 8 May 2017, unreported.

[111] Article 827 JC.

[112] Article 1017 JC.

[113] Article 1018 JC.

to the award of costs for technical assistance in favour of Telenet. Also, since UVP had not raised any objections to the cost of technical assistance, the Court of Appeal decided that it could be assumed that all the costs claimed were directly and closely linked to the proceedings, sparing the Court of Appeal the assessment of the nature of the costs claimed for by Telenet. Telenet was awarded 63.804,25 EUR.

1.3.1.4 A Number of Brief Considerations Regarding the Influence of EU Case Law

These two examples on the interaction between EU law and national civil procedure allow for a number of brief considerations.

First, the Court's decisions will be relevant for the internal Belgian debate regarding the *ex officio* powers of judges in default proceedings and the reimbursement of expert fees. It is very likely that the solutions provided for in the case law of the Court will inform a future procedural framework encompassing both EU law and purely national law cases. Why allow a judge sitting in default proceedings only to apply *ex officio* EU consumer law and not national consumer law, or any other area of law? That will be a tough question to answer. The same goes for the regime applicable to the reimbursement of expert fees. The decision by the Antwerp Court of Appeal implies that the rules regarding the reimbursement of fees for party-appointed experts have now been changed for litigation falling within the scope of the IPED. The question is whether the Belgian courts will henceforth maintain a separate regime for IP litigation or whether the ruling of the Court of Justice will also create effects in other areas of law. Also, will the legislator react? It is instructive in this regard to refer to the preparatory works of the Belgian legislator on the implementation of the IPED. During the debate a number of procedural issues were raised that required particular attention in light of the IPED: the reimbursement of lawyers' fees and the protection of confidential evidence. The legislator did, however, not act upon these issues in the context of the transposition of the IPED because it preferred a horizontal approach, regulating the matter for the whole of civil procedure instead of providing a separate regime for IP litigation.[114]

In regard of the reimbursement of lawyers' fees, a law was enacted shortly later regulating the matter for the whole of civil litigation.[115] When the legislator's preference for a horizontal approach would equally find application regarding the issue of the reimbursement of party-appointed experts, which is a credible assumption in light of how it addressed the reimbursement of lawyers' fees, the judgment of the Court of Justice may have consequences far beyond the scope of the IPED and EU law. Indeed, when remaining faithful to its horizontal approach to the regulation of civil procedure, the Belgian legislator would effectively have to

[114] Chamber of Representatives 2006–2007, Preparatory Works N° 2943/001, p. 18.

[115] Van Drooghenbroeck and De Coninck 2008, pp. 37–60.

incorporate the standard laid down in the *Telenet* judgment in its rules on the reimbursement of party-appointed experts.

Second, the discussion regarding the *ex officio* application of the UCTD and the recent amendments to default proceedings in Belgium demonstrate the relevance of EU law for civil procedure reforms in the Member States. A problem may thus arise where a national legislator fails to take into account the EU law dimension when enacting rules on national civil procedure. The Belgian case is a clear illustration of ignorance or negligence on part of the legislator, the amendment solely focusing on the national debate on default proceedings.[116] A national legislator can, however, not ignore the EU law dimension and should assess on any occasion the potential EU law impact. Rules of civil procedure are not solely concerned with the application of national law.

The failure to take the EU law dimension into account should neither be considered to be an unfortunate oversight. It leads to the obstruction of an important EU policy priority, making the State susceptible to infringement proceedings by the European Commission. It may also strengthen the case for EU action in matters of civil procedure. In the end, a legislator that is not willing to take into account the EU law dimension in the context of civil procedure may risk losing its power to regulate all together.

1.3.2 EU Rules on Civil Procedure

1.3.2.1 Introduction

The focus of the European Commission in a number of policy areas has recently shifted from substantive regulation to enforcement. A good example is the field of consumer protection law. The 2017 Report on the Fitness Check of consumer and marketing law states that the existing body of substantive consumer law is largely sufficient but that major challenges exist when it comes to enforcement.[117] An important part of the imminent consumer law reform will therefore concern rules on the enforcement of substantive consumer law.[118]

The suggested policy options in the Report on the Fitness Check seem to focus on private enforcement, which is in line with the general approach the European Commission takes in consumer law matters.[119] Potential initiatives will focus on improving access to redress by consumers, both individually and collectively.[120] To

[116] Justice of the Peace Westerlo, 2 March 2016, Rechtskundig Weekblad 2016–2017, 273.

[117] European Commission, Report on the Fitness Check on various consumer law directives, SWD (2017) 209 final, p. 76 (hereafter 'Report on the Fitness Check').

[118] Report on the Fitness Check, p. 85.

[119] Wilman 2015, p. 417.

[120] Report on the Fitness Check, p. 77.

name a few: individual EU-wide rights to remedies to challenge violations of the Unfair Commercial Practices Directive,[121] guidance regarding the *ex officio* application of the UCTD[122] and adaptations to the Injunctions Directive.[123] Civil procedure laws of the Member States may thus be affected.[124]

The policy choice for private enforcement has an important impact on national civil procedure, for enforcement by private parties will largely take place before civil courts through damages actions, injunctions or contractual remedies. Further to this, a trend of private enforcement is not only present in consumer law.[125] The same goes for discrimination law[126] or competition law.[127] It can thus be expected that this general trend will entail further consequences for Member State civil procedure in the future.

In the next two subheadings I will illustrate the implications of the trend towards regulating enforcement by briefly analysing the impact of the Private Damages Directive and the Trade Secrets Directive in the Belgian legal order on a number of points.

1.3.2.2 Private Damages Directive

General

On 26 November 2014, the Council and the European Parliament adopted a directive regulating certain aspects of private damages claims for violations of EU and national competition law.[128] The Private Damages Directive (hereafter 'PDD') has multiple aims: allowing victims of competition law infringements to seek damages, providing a credible private enforcement complement to public enforcement and to create extra dissuasive effect vis-à-vis potential infringers.[129] The directive entered into force in 2014[130] with a deadline for transposition by the end of 2016.[131] It harmonises a number of important issues regarding damages actions for competition law infringements. The directive does, however, not

121 Report on the Fitness Check, p. 77.

122 Report on the Fitness Check, p. 77.

123 Report on the Fitness Check, p. 78.

124 On 11 April 2018, the European Commission adopted a proposal for a directive on a consumer collective redress mechanism. This would introduce a collective redress mechanism in all EU Member States if adopted by the EU legislator. See COM(2018) 184 final.

125 Jauering and Hess 2011, p. 3.

126 Kilpatrick 2001, p. 147.

127 Wilman 2015, pp. 202–220.

128 Directive 2010/104/EU of the European Parliament and of the Council of 26 November 2014 on certain rules governing actions for damages under national law for infringements of the competition law provisions of the Member States and of the European Union, *O.J.* 2014, L 349/1.

129 Recitals 5 and 6 PDD.

130 Article 23 PDD.

131 Article 21 PDD.

introduce the remedy as such in the EU Member States. The Court of Justice had already decided in 2001 that such actions must be available in all Member States.[132]

The PDD contains a number of procedural provisions that allow for the proper functioning of a private damages action in the field of competition law. It lays down a principle of full compensation[133] and deals notably with disclosure of evidence and the powers of national courts to order such disclosure,[134] the effects of decisions of (foreign) competition authorities and foreign courts in national court proceedings,[135] limitation periods,[136] and rules on the effect of consensual dispute resolution on court proceedings.[137] Further to this, it regulates issues of joined and several liability,[138] the passing-on defence,[139] the rights of indirect purchasers,[140] the possibility of a multitude of claims,[141] and the quantification of harm.[142] In regard of this last issue the directive lays down a rebuttable presumption that cartel infringements cause harm.[143] Lastly, it should be pointed out that the directive also applies to national competition law where this is applied in parallel to EU competition law.[144]

Impact in Belgium

The directive was implemented by a law of 6 June 2017, which entered into force on 22 June 2017.[145] It is worth noting that the relevant procedural provisions have not been inserted in the Judicial Code but in a separate Title of Book XVII of the Code of Economic Law.[146] The impact on Belgian procedural law has multiple aspects. I will focus on the rules of prescription and the presumption of harm.

---

[132] Judgment of 20 September 2001, *Courage and Crehan*, C-453/99, EU:C:2001:465, para 26.

[133] Article 3 PDD.

[134] Articles 6–8 PDD.

[135] Article 9 PDD.

[136] Article 10 PDD.

[137] Articles 18–19 PDD.

[138] Article 11 PDD.

[139] Articles 12–13 PDD.

[140] Article 14 PDD.

[141] Article 15 PDD.

[142] Article 17 PDD.

[143] Article 17(2) PDD.

[144] Recital 9 and Article 2(1) PDD.

[145] Law of 6 June 2017 on the insertion of Title 3 "The claim for damages for violations of competition law" in Book XVII of the Code of Economic Law, on the insertion of definitions proper to Book XVII, Title 3 in Book I, and on various amendments of the Code of Economic Law, Belgian State Gazette 12 June 2017, p. 63596 (available online from http://www.ejustice.just.fgov.be/eli/loi/2017/06/06/2017012339/moniteur).

[146] The Code of Economic Law gradually entered progressively into force from 31 May 2014 onwards. It encompasses 18 books regulating various aspects of the economic life, from consumer law to competition law and IP law.

Rules on Prescription

The directive had already a first impact in the Belgian legal order during the deadline for transposition, namely regarding the point of departure of the limitation period for damages actions.

A first instance judge confronted with a private damages claim of an undertaking against a competitor on account of a violation of competition law referred a preliminary question to the Belgian Constitutional Court on the application of the rule contained in Article 2262bis, § 1(2) Civil Code.[147] That provision states that a claim for damages on the basis of extra-contractual liability is prescribed five years from the day following the day on which the victim gained knowledge of the damage or its increase, and of the identity of the responsible person. It should be pointed out that in the case at hand an investigation was taking place by the Belgian competition authorities into the violation of the rules on competition. However, due to the length of the administrative investigation by the competition authorities it was unlikely that the final decision could be used as evidence in the damages action. The referring court asked the Belgian Constitutional Court whether it was compatible with the Constitution that an investigation of the competition authorities did not lead to a suspension or interruption of the limitation period for bringing a damages action.

In its reasoning, the Constitutional Court paid particular attention to the difficult position in which private parties find themselves when seeking to prove a violation of competition law. It expressly referred to the need for a complex factual and economic analysis and the fact that the required evidence is often not publicly available.[148] The standard of evidence required would thus make it very difficult for private parties to meet the burden of proof. That is, however, less the case for the competition authorities, according to the Constitutional Court. They have the necessary means and extensive powers of investigation to obtain the required evidence.[149] The Constitutional Court appreciated this reality and appears to have inferred from this that parties in competition damages claims will often have to rely on an administrative decision of a competition authority to establish a violation of competition law.[150]

The applicable rules on prescription, however, did not necessarily allow this. Moreover, the absence of a suspension or an interruption of the limitation period pending the outcome of administrative proceedings would force a party to start civil proceedings in order to safeguard its claim, even before a violation of competition law would be established by the competition authorities. Such uncertainty would entail a serious risk for that party, as it may be exposed to costs in case the authorities would in the end not establish a violation of competition law or would

---

[147] Belgian Constitutional Court 10 March 2016, N° 38/2016 (available online from http://www.const-court.be/public/n/2016/2016-038n.pdf).

[148] Belgian Constitutional Court 10 March 2016, N° 38/2016, B.9.

[149] Belgian Constitutional Court 10 March 2016, N° 38/2016, B.9.

[150] Belgian Constitutional Court 10 March 2016, N° 38/2016, B.12.

only establish a violation after the damages action has been concluded.[151] The Constitutional Court considered this to be a serious impediment to exercise of the right to damages for violations of competition law. Consequently, it concluded that the lack of suspension or interruption of the limitation period pending the outcome of the investigation of the competition authorities is contrary to the Constitution.[152]

The Constitutional Court only refers in a subsidiary manner to the Private Damages Directive, underlining that the outcome of its decision is *also* envisaged in the directive.[153] The decision appears thus to be primarily based on Belgian constitutional law. However, a closer look at the reasoning of the Constitutional Court suggests that the PDD had a much greater influence on the decision than what appears from the judgment. The reasoning regarding the problems faced by an applicant in proving a competition law infringement corresponds almost literally to the text of the PDD, especially recital 14 PDD. The Constitutional Court equally subscribes to the view expressed in recital 26 PDD, that competition damages claims are essentially follow-up actions. Moreover, the decision of the Constitutional Court corresponds almost exactly to the rule laid down in Article 10(4) PDD, namely that:

> Member States shall ensure that a limitation period is suspended or, depending on national law, interrupted, if a competition authority takes action for the purpose of the investigation or its proceedings in respect of an infringement of competition law to which the action for damages relates. The suspension shall end at the earliest one year after the infringement decision has become final or after the proceedings are otherwise terminated.[154]

The striking similarities make it difficult to maintain that the judgment was only based on Belgian constitutional law. The fact that the implementation period of the PDD had not elapsed at the time of the judgment, as well as the fact that the actual case dated from before the adoption of the PDD may explain why the Constitutional Court only made a minimal reference to the PDD.

It is interesting to compare the approach taken by the Belgian Constitutional Court to that of the Italian Supreme Court. In its judgment of 4 June 2015, the latter quashed a decision of the Rome Court of Appeal for a failure to interpret the rules on evidence in line with the principle of effective judicial protection.[155] The Italian Supreme Court reasoned that follow-up actions for private damages would be deprived of their effectiveness if the ordinary rules on the burden of proof were followed, given the difficulties for private parties to obtain the required proof. The case concerned the issue of information asymmetry between the applicant and the defendant and the powers of courts to overcome such asymmetry. It should be

---

[151] Belgian Constitutional Court 10 March 2016, N° 38/2016, B.13.

[152] Belgian Constitutional Court 10 March 2016, N° 38/2016, B.14. For a similar problem in the German legal order, see Federal Court of Justice (BGH), judgment of 12 June 2018, KZR 56/16 – *Grauzementkartell II*.

[153] Belgian Constitutional Court 10 March 2016, N° 38/2016, B.12.

[154] With the entry into force of the Belgian law implementing the Private Damages Directive, such an interruption can now also be found in Article XVII.90 Code of Economic Law.

[155] Italian Supreme Court, N° 11564/2015, 4 June 2015, IT:CASS:2015:11564CIV.

recalled that this issue is addressed in the PDD, by obliging the Member States to lay down a specific disclosure regime.[156] The Supreme Court reproached the appeal court to have applied the existing rules on the burden of proof in a mechanical way instead of using its powers of instruction to collect the necessary information from the defending party.[157] According to the Supreme Court, such approach did not take into account the specific circumstances of the case and did not lead to an effective application of EU competition law.

Contrary to the Belgian Constitutional Court, the Italian Supreme Court relied on EU law to give effect to the PDD. It interpreted the Treaty provisions on competition law, the right to damages enshrined therein, and the right to effective judicial protection as laid down in the Charter and Article 19 TEU in light of the PDD and concluded that EU law required the taking of measures of inquiry.[158] It thus found a direct basis in EU law to apply the PDD prematurely instead of relying mainly on national law to secure the effective application of competition law.[159] While the approach of the Italian Supreme Court is more transparent as it makes the influence of EU law clearly visible, both cases equally illustrate how EU considerations regarding the effective application of EU competition law find their ways into the national legal order.

Presumption of Harm

A presumption of a causal link between a violation of the law and harm does not exist in Belgian liability law. In accordance with the general rules of evidence, it is for the claimant to prove that harm has actually occurred as a result of a violation of the law.[160] This issue came to haunt the European Commission when it attempted to obtain damages from the members of the elevator cartel.[161]

In a follow-up action to the finding of a violation of competition law established by the European Commission,[162] the European Commission filed a damages claim against the members of the elevator cartel in the Brussels Commercial Court.[163]

---

[156] Article 5 PDD.

[157] 'Questo metodo non è stato seguito dai giudici di merito, i quali, come detto (al par. 3.3), hanno deciso la causa applicando meccanicamente il principio dell'onere della prova, senza valutare l'opportunità di attivare i poteri istruttori anche d'ufficio e mostrando di non cogliere la specifica peculiarità della controversia.'

[158] See Gualco and Lourenço 2016, pp. 648–650 on interpreting a general principle in light of a directive.

[159] Note that the Court of Justice has reinforced this way of reasoning in a recent decision. See Judgment of 17 April 2018, *Egenberger*, C-414/16, EU:C:2018:257.

[160] Article 1315 Civil Code and Article 870 Judicial Code.

[161] Brussels Commercial Court, 24 November 2014, available in Dutch at http://ec.europa.eu/competition/national_courts/cases/143115/143115_1_3.pdf.

[162] European Commission, Decision of 21 February 2007 relating to a proceeding under Article 81 of the EC Treaty: Case COMP/E-1/38.823 – PO/Elevators and Escalators, C (2007) 512 final.

[163] It should be pointed out that such a case does not come within the jurisdiction of the Court of Justice of the European Union.

It argued, *inter alia*, that no causal link should be proven between a cartel infringement and harm since it can be presumed that harm has occurred. However, the Brussels Commercial Court rejected the argument, holding that such a presumption did not exist in Belgian law. It also rejected the argument to read Belgian procedural law in conformity with the Private Damages Directive, in particular with the rule contained in Article 17(2) PDD. This provision states that '[i]t shall be presumed that cartel infringements cause harm'. The judge held that the Directive had not yet been implemented and that the damages action was brought well before the Private Damages Directive had been adopted. Consequently, the European Commission's claim was rejected. The Brussels Commercial Court could, however, have taken a different approach, similar to the approach taken by the Italian Supreme Court in its judgment of 4 June 2015. It could have reasoned that the Directive was merely a concretisation of the right to damages for the violation of competition rules as laid down by the Court of Justice in its judgments in *Courage and Crehan*[164] and *Manfredi*,[165] the exercise of such right being extremely difficult or virtually impossible in absence of a presumption of a causal link between a competition law infringement and harm.[166] The case is now pending before the Brussels Court of Appeal.

Whatever the outcome of the appeal case may be, the conclusion reached by the Brussels Commercial Court is henceforth no longer possible. With the implementation of the Private Damages Directive, a provision was inserted in the Code of Economic Law creating a rebuttable presumption of a causal connection between a cartel infringement and harm.[167]

1.3.2.3 Trade Secrets Directive

General

On 8 June 2016, the EU legislator adopted the Trade Secrets Directive (TSD).[168] The goal of the directive is to approximate the laws of the Member States in order to ensure that there is a sufficient and consistent level of civil redress in the internal market in the event of unlawful acquisition, use or disclosure of a trade secret.[169]

Article 6 TSD lays down a general obligation to provide effective remedies against the unlawful acquisition, use and disclosure of trade secrets. The directive then continues with a number of specific rules regarding limitation periods,[170] the

---

164 Judgment of 20 September 2001, *Courage and Crehan*, C-453/99, EU:C:2001:465, para 26.

165 Judgment of 13 July 2006, *Manfredi*, C-295/04 to C-298/04, EU:C:2006:461, para 60.

166 Cfr. the approach taken by the Italian Supreme Court. See also Judgment of 17 April 2018, *Egenberger*, C-414/16, EU:C:2018:257

167 Article XVII.73 Code of Economic Law.

168 Directive (EU) 2016/943 of the European Parliament and of the Council of 8 June 2016 on the protection of undisclosed know-how and business information (trade secrets) against their unlawful acquisition, use and disclosure, *O.J.* 2016, L 157/1.

169 Recital 10 TSD.

170 Article 8 TSD.

preservation of confidentiality of trade secrets in the course of legal proceedings,[171] provisional and precautionary measures,[172] injunctive and corrective measures,[173] damages,[174] and publication of judicial decisions.[175] The Private Damages Directive is thus not an exception on account of the specific situation of competition law, but the emanation of a more general trend to intervene actively in matters of enforcement.

Impact in Belgium

The Trade Secrets Directive should only be implemented in the legal orders of the Member States by 9 June 2018.[176] It is therefore too early to comment on the implementation process in Belgium. Yet, it is possible to look at the current legal landscape and to signal a number of issues that potentially require particular attention of the Belgian legislator.

Remedies and Their Scope

The directive strengthens the protection of business secrets both by extending the scope of existing remedies and by introducing new remedies. A first innovation concerns the circle of potential parties against whom an action for damages can be brought. At present, a majority of Belgian legal doctrine considers that a cessation order is only possible against the divulgation of a business secret but not against its use. This means that users can in principle not be required to stop using an illegally divulged business secret.[177] The directive will enlarge the scope of protection, providing for a strong basis to act against third parties who benefited from the divulgation of business secrets.[178] A second improvement concerns the available remedies for victims of an act of divulgation. At present, the focus in Belgium lies on the act of divulgation, which can be subject to interim measures, orders of cessation and contractual or extra-contractual liability. However, a conservatory measure or a coercive measure against (new) products produced on the basis of illegally divulged business secrets does currently not exist in Belgian law.[179] The

[171] Article 9 TSD.

[172] Article 10 TSD.

[173] Article 12 TSD.

[174] Article 14 TSD.

[175] Article 15 TSD.

[176] Article 19(1) TSD. Note that a proposal for an implementing law was only laid before the Belgian Parliament on 12 June 2018. See http://www.dekamer.be/kvvcr/showpage.cfm?section=/flwb&language=fr&cfm=/site/wwwcfm/flwb/flwbn.cfm?legislist=legisnr&dossierID=3154

[177] Dupont 2016, p. 153.

[178] Article 4(5) TSD.

[179] Dupont 2016, p. 154. It does exist in the context of IP enforcement against forgeries, but not in the context of the protection of business secrets.

directive explicitly provides for such measures,[180] allowing a victim of the divulgation of business secrets to target the fruits of the divulged secret information.

New remedies are thus effectively being introduced in the Belgian legal order on the basis of an EU directive. This could not be further away from the early decisions of the Court of Justice on national procedural law, in which it stated that it was not the intention of the EU Treaties to introduce new remedies in the legal orders of the Member States.[181]

Protection of Confidentiality in the Course of Judicial Proceedings

Another issue is the protection of business secrets in the course of judicial proceedings. An applicant seeking protection of its business secrets may have to prove that (a) a trade secret exists, (b) that he is the trade secret holder, and (c) the trade secret has been acquired unlawfully, is being unlawfully used or disclosed, or unlawful acquisition, use or disclosure of the trade secret is imminent.[182] This means that trade secrets may become part of the evidence that is necessary to substantiate a claim to seek protection of those trade secrets. The question is whether access to evidence in this regard may be restricted, requiring a court to strike a balance between the right to a fair trial and the protection of trade secrets. This issue has not been specifically regulated in the Belgian Judicial Code and the protection of business secrets depends currently on court practice. Judges have provided for *ad hoc* mechanisms to balance the right to a fair trial and the protection of business secrets but unfortunately there is no real consistency.[183] The TSD now requires the Belgian legislator to provide for a coherent legal framework, based on the detailed rules laid down in the directive.[184]

1.3.2.4 A Number of Brief Considerations Regarding the Influence of EU Legislation

The two directives serve as apt illustrations on various points of the approach taken to civil procedure at the level of the EU. A first thing that can be noticed is that the distinction between procedural law and substantive law is not clearly made.[185] The PDD contains a number of rules that would qualify as rules of substantive law from a Member State perspective. The blurring of procedural law and substantive law is, however, typical for the broad approach to procedural law taken at EU level.

---

[180] Articles 10(1)(c) and 12(2)(c) TSD.

[181] Judgment of 7 July 1981, *Rewe-Handelsgesellschaft Nord*, 158/80, EU:C:1981:163, para 44.

[182] Article 11(1) TSD.

[183] Dupont 2016, pp. 154–156.

[184] Article 9(2) TSD.

[185] On the distinction between procedural and substantive law, see Halpérin and Niboyet 2014, pp. 5–27. For a historical perspective, see Van Caenegem 2002, pp. 48–50.

The debate on the effectiveness of national civil procedure at EU level involves every element that impacts on the possibility to enforce EU law rights before national courts, regardless of their nature. Also the Court of Justice applies the principle of effectiveness to matters that will be considered as being part of substantive law in some Member States, for example limitation periods. To paraphrase Van Gerven on this point: procedural law regulation at EU level encompasses both procedural rules *sensu stricto* and remedial rules.[186]

Second, both directives provide for a specific procedural framework for a specific substantive law context. This is characteristic of the approach to procedural law regulation at EU level. Procedural rules are devised to deal with a specific problem and are not part of a general legislative framework for procedural law. Even between European instruments differences exist in regard of solutions provided for similar problems. For example, the issue of the use of confidential information in the course of civil proceedings is dealt with differently in both directives.[187] This tailor-made approach to the regulation of procedural law also impacts upon the fabric of national civil procedure. The implementation of the PDD in Belgium—but also Germany—has resulted in a specific procedural framework for disclosure proceedings tailored to damages actions for competition law infringements, departing from the general approach to disclosure in national civil procedure.

Third, a procedural issue dealt with in an EU directive related to a specific substantive law context may generate wider effects in the national system of civil procedure. A good example is the protection of business secrets in civil litigation. It should be recalled that there is currently no clear framework for such protection in Belgium. The matter was discussed during the process of implementation of the IP enforcement directive. The protection of secret knowhow is indeed a point of particular salience in IP litigation. The Belgian legislator did not take up the matter, however, explicitly stating that the issue should be regulated in a horizontal manner, not only in relation to IP litigation.[188] A separate legislative proposal on the matter was never considered. The TSD will oblige the Belgian legislator to take this matter up again.[189] If the legislator would stick to its 2006 position, the implementation of the TSD will lead to the enactment of a general regime for the protection of business secrets in civil litigation. It is an illustration of how specific EU procedural rules may provoke a much wider reform of national civil procedure, beyond the matter for the purposes of which the Directive was adopted. Conversely, the implementation of the PDD has demonstrated that the Belgian legislator is not always coherent in its horizontal approach to civil procedure. EU rules on civil procedure thus seem to provoke a difficult choice between horizontality and specificity.

---

[186] Van Gerven 2000, pp. 522–525.

[187] Compare Article 9(2) TSD to Article 5(4) PDD.

[188] Chamber of Representatives 2006–2007, Preparatory Works N° 2943/001, p. 15.

[189] Article 9(2) TSD.

1.4 Different Approaches to Civil Procedure

In the previous part I have illustrated the impact of EU law on national civil procedure, more specifically Belgian civil procedure, with a number of examples originating in the case law of the Court of Justice and in EU legislation. The aim of this section is to provide for more general considerations regarding the impact of EU law on national civil procedure on the basis of these examples.

1.4.1 EU Approach to Civil Procedure: Sectoral and Functional

What appears from section three is that the EU enacts rules of civil procedure with a view to reinforce the application of specific substantive rules: the Private Damages Directive lays down procedural rules that contribute to the enforcement of competition law; the IP Enforcement Directive lays down rules that contribute to the enforcement of IP law; the case law of the Court of Justice regarding the *ex officio* application of the UCTD specifically contributes to the effective application of the latter; and the Trade Secrets Directive lays down procedural rules tailored to the protection of trade secrets. Also, it should be noted that procedural frameworks differ between directives, even when they regulate a largely similar issue. For example, regarding the disclosure of evidence, the TSD provides for a specific framework for the preservation of confidentiality of trade secrets in the course of legal proceedings relating to the unlawful acquisition, use or disclosure of a trade secret,[190] whereas the PDD merely states that

> Member States shall ensure that national courts have the power to order the disclosure of evidence containing confidential information where they consider it relevant to the action for damages. Member States shall ensure that, when ordering the disclosure of such information, national courts have at their disposal effective measures to protect such information.[191]

There appears to be no coordination between the two directives whereas the procedural issue is largely similar, namely the protection of confidential information in the course of legal proceedings, which may include trade secrets. What kind of framework should a Member State provide in order to safeguard the confidential nature of evidence containing trade secrets in the context a damages action for competition law infringements? Should it apply a national procedural solution, adopted in exercise of the discretion left to it by the PDD, or by way of analogy, the specific framework of the TSD?

---

[190] Article 9 TSD.

[191] Article 5 PDD.

The issue is characteristic of civil procedure of EU law origin: a rule of civil procedure is not embedded in a general and coherent framework, but it is tailored to the specific substantive law context in which it has been enacted. Civil procedure at EU level is thus both sectoral and functional: it differentiates between substantive law areas and even between instruments within a specific area (sectoral) and provides a specific procedural solution to contribute to the application and enforcement of a specific substantive issue (functional).[192]

The sectoral and functional approach to civil procedure can be explained by going back to the basic architecture of the European Union.[193] The EU is a functional international organisation, upon which competences have been conferred to realise a number of policy objectives. This transpires from Article 5(2) TEU, which states that "the Union shall act only within the limits of the competences conferred upon it by the Member States in the Treaties to attain the objectives set out therein". This is called the principle of conferral.[194] It can explain to a large extent why the EU's approach to national civil procedure is sectoral and functional.

The EU Member States have not conferred upon the EU a general competence to enact rules of civil procedure.[195] This means that a general law on civil procedure cannot currently be enacted at EU level.[196] However, it does not mean that the EU has no competence for harmonising rules of civil procedure. Each substantive law competence conferred upon the EU implies the competence to lay down rules that facilitate the enforcement of rules enacted on the basis of that head of competence.[197] Such rules may include rules of civil procedure. This can be illustrated by the PDD and the TSD, which are based on the EU's competence for competition policy and internal market policy. Rules of civil procedure thus find their origin in a competence for conducting a substantive policy, not in a competence for procedure. On that basis many other procedural rules have been enacted by the EU legislator. I have already mentioned the IPED, the PDD, the TSD and the Injunctions Directive. Another good example is the Public Procurement Remedies Directives,[198] providing a specific procedural framework for remedies in the

---

[192] Krans 2010, pp. 163–164; Kilpatrick 2001, pp. 175–176.

[193] Every discussion on EU law can ultimately be traced back to a constitutional issue.

[194] See Schütze 2015, pp. 224–225.

[195] I do not take into account rules for cross-border procedures in this respect.

[196] Hess 2010, p. 75.

[197] Adinolfi 2012, p. 303.

[198] Council Directive 89/665/EEC of 21 December 1989 on the coordination of the laws, regulations and administrative provisions relating to the application of review procedures to the award of public supply and public works contracts, *O.J.* 1989, L 395/33 and Council Directive 92/13/EEC of 25 February 1992 coordinating the laws, regulations and administrative provisions relating to the application of Community rules on the procurement procedures of entities operating in the water, energy, transport and telecommunications sectors, *O.J.* 1992, L 76/14, as (substantially) amended by Directive 2007/66/EC of the European Parliament and of the Council of 11 December 2007 amending Council Directives 89/665/EEC and 92/13/EEC with regard to improving the effectiveness of review procedures concerning the award of public contracts, *O.J.* 2007, L 335/31, and subsequent amendments.

context of public procurement law. The principle of conferral in combination with the absence of a general head of competence for civil procedure explains thus why the EU's approach to procedural law is sectoral.

The principle of conferral can also explain the functional approach to civil procedure. Competences have been conferred upon the EU to contribute to the realisation of a number of policy objectives.[199] When the EU enacts a piece of legislation on the basis of a competence conferred upon it, it must make sure that such legislation contributes to the realisation of the objectives for the purposes of which that competence has been conferred upon the EU. Given the fact that the EU's competence for civil procedure is implicit in a substantive policy competence, the rules of civil procedure it enacts on the basis of such a competence heading must therefore contribute to the realisation of the policy objectives connected to that competence. Procedural rules enacted on the basis of the EU's competence for consumer policy must contribute to the EU's consumer policy; procedural rules enacted on the basis of the EU's competence for competition policy must contribute to the EU's competition policy; etc. Wagner calls this the 'Materialisierung' of civil procedure.[200]

Note in this regard that the Court of Justice substantiates its decision in *United Video Properties* by referring to the dissuasive effect that Article 14 IPED must have on infringers of the rights of a rightholder.[201] It is the perfect illustration of how the goal of the actual directive informs the Court's interpretation of Article 14 IPED, and not (solely) a procedural access to justice approach.[202] This is even more visible in the case law of the Court of Justice concerning the *ex officio* application of the UCTD. The *ex officio* application is a procedural tool to ensure that the UCTD is actually being applied and that its policy goals can be realised.[203] The potential disturbing effect of its case law on the established division of tasks between judges and parties in national civil procedure does not appear to be a point of major concern to the Court. The functional approach to civil procedure makes procedural considerations largely ancillary to substantive law concerns.[204]

It should be pointed out that the same applies where the EU legislator has not laid down procedural rules, but the Court is required to assess whether national procedural law allows for the effective application of a rule of EU substantive law. The Court will interpret the effectiveness requirement in light of the goals of EU substantive law and assess whether national civil procedure contributes to those goals. The functional approach to civil procedure also applies in a pure national procedural autonomy context.

---

[199] Article 3(6) TEU.

[200] Wagner 2008, p. 18.

[201] *United Video Properties*, para 27.

[202] Adinolfi 2012, pp. 299–300.

[203] *Asbeek Brusse*, paras 54–60.

[204] Kakouris 1997, p. 1406.

1.4.2 Member State Approach to Civil Procedure: Horizontal and Autonomous

The sectoral and functional approach to civil procedure at EU level contrasts with the approach typically taken at national level, which is horizontal and more autonomous. I mean by this that civil procedure at the national level provides in principle for a uniform and coherent procedural framework that applies throughout civil procedure. Further to this, civil procedure is not specifically tailored to particular substantive law needs but has its own logic. It has an autonomous character[205] and is not considered to be a mere accessory to substantive law. An explanation for such different approach to civil procedure can be found in the different regulatory context at the level of the Member States, especially the context existing at the turn of the 19th century, when the foundations for current continental civil procedure were laid.

A state was considered to be sovereign and to exercise unlimited authority over its territory.[206] This entailed that the state had a general competence to regulate and was not functionally limited in the exercise of its competences.[207] It is exactly the absence of those two elements that currently prevents the EU from enacting a general instrument on civil procedure. The 19th century nation state, however, had all the power to enact a horizontal framework of civil procedure. The question is why it did so. Legal historians point at the drive to centralise power at the level of the central state.[208] Legislation in this regard was as much about regulating as about creating and strengthening new-born nation states.[209] This implied a move towards uniformity and coherence, doing away with the localism that was still widespread at the time.[210] Furthermore, one could point at the concern of equality and how civil procedure should apply in an equal fashion to everyone.[211] The upshot was a codification movement,[212] which sought to provide for a closed and coherent set of rules for every area of law within a given state. This resulted in the adoption of codes in various areas of law, of which the French *Code de procédure civile* is probably the most telling example from the point of view of civil procedure. Many other EU Member States provided for a code of civil procedure around that time or shortly after. Also former Soviet States followed this approach after the fall of the

[205] Sobrie 2016, p. 46; de Leval 2015, pp. 15–16.

[206] Loughlin 2013, p. 34.

[207] Walker 2013, p. 20.

[208] Zimmermann 2003, p. 19; Van Caenegem 1992, pp. 125–126.

[209] Kroppenberg and Linder 2014, pp. 80–81. See in this regard the famous statement of Portalis, one of the fathers of the French Civil Code: "Today, uniform legislation has made all the absurdities and dangers disappear; civil order has cemented the political order. We will no longer be Provencal, Bretons, Alsatians, but French." Cited in Kroppenberg and Linder 2014, p. 78.

[210] Wijffels 2008, pp. 6 and 16–17.

[211] Wieacker 1974, p. 80; Rubenstein 2001–2002, pp. 1884 et seq.

[212] Zimmermann 2003, pp. 18–19.

Berlin Wall.[213] The result is that national civil procedure has been largely uniformised in almost all continental systems.[214]

The choice for a code as an instrument of regulation is not without consequences. A code typically provides for a uniform and coherent system of principles and rules for a given area of law.[215] Such is inherent in the concept of codification.[216] This means that it is often a daunting task to amend a code, as piecemeal modifications risk distorting the balance created by the code.[217] It explains why codes are not easily replaced. They effectively buttress the law for a long period of time[218] and have a profound impact on future legal practice and thinking.[219]

The origins of modern civil procedure are thus still indebted to the drive for uniformity existing at the time. Moreover, uniformity and coherence continue to be important values of civil procedure in the 21st century. Leading civil procedure scholars in France and Belgium have stated that fragmentation should be exceptional and is not preferable.[220] The spirit of codification has survived.[221] This is what I characterise as a horizontal approach to civil procedure.

An apt illustration of such horizontal approach is the debate on the implementation of the IPED in Belgium. It should be recalled that both reimbursement of lawyers' fees as well as the protection of confidential evidence was not properly regulated in Belgium at that time. These issues were raised by some members of the Belgian parliament because the IPED potentially required legislative action in this regard. The Belgian legislator explicitly stated, however, that it did not want to include rules on those matters in the law implementing the IPED because it wanted to lay down a general framework for these matters, applying throughout the whole of civil procedure.[222] It specifically referred to the 'horizontal nature' of these issues.

Also, having a competence to enact procedural rules detached from the competence to enact substantive law, it is more likely that a State will see civil procedure as a distinct set of rules with its own policy goals. Such policy goals are usually of a general nature,[223] contributing to the realisation of the public service of

[213] Zimmermann 2003, p. 19.

[214] Zimmermann 2003, p. 19.

[215] Cfr. Zimmermann 2014, pp. 13–14; Van Caenegem 1992, pp. 11–14.

[216] Chadelat 2006, p. 50; Sobrie 2016, p. 30.

[217] Caenegem 1992, p. 14.

[218] Codifications are dominated by a notion of timelessness: Chadelat 2006, p. 50.

[219] See for example the impact of the French Code of Civil Procedure on Belgian civil procedure: Wijffels 2008, pp. 52–54.

[220] Cadiet 2006, pp. 7–8; Laenens et al. 2016, p. 18–19. Whether coherence is actually achieved in practice is a different point. What matters for our discussion is that coherence is considered as a guiding normative principle. On the distinction between coherence as an empirical reality and a normative principle, see Rödl 2015, pp. 38–41.

[221] Cfr. Van Caenegem 2002, p. 22.

[222] Chamber of Representatives 2006–2007, Preparatory Works N° 2943/001, pp. 15 and 18.

[223] See, for example, Van Orshoven 2016, p. 160; Genn 2010, pp. 1–26; Woolf 1996, § 1.

justice.[224] The application of substantive law must thus be realised against the backdrop of an overarching justice policy, which means that substantive law has to subscribe to a procedural logic in order to be applied and enforced. Procedural law is largely autonomous[225] in such a context and cannot be bended every time this would serve the better realisation of the goals of substantive law. It is 'trans-substantive'[226] and has its own internal logic.[227] The functional idea of procedural law is thus lacking in this respect, apart from the general goal of procedural law to facilitate access to justice.

1.5 Consequences for Civil Procedure at the Member State Level

It appears from the previous section that the regulatory context provides for an explanation for the different approaches to civil procedure. The different approach to civil procedure at EU level (sectoral/functional) is, however, not without consequences for the organisation of civil procedure at Member State level (horizontal/autonomous). The interaction between two different conceptions of civil procedure may lead to fragmentation of civil procedure and/or a loss of national regulatory powers in the field of civil procedure.

1.5.1 The Issue of Fragmentation

The specific procedural regimes created at EU level challenge the traditional uniform conception of civil procedure.[228] The horizontal approach is being departed from in favour of a sectoral approach following which procedural design is adapted to substantive goals. This is a major development as it challenges many years of conceptual thinking about civil procedure, based on general principles and adherence to coherence. It triggers a 'decodification' of civil procedure and diminishes the autonomous nature of civil procedure. The issue was raised by the Advocate General in *United Video Properties*, who stated that the sectoral approach to civil procedure at EU level can lead to "the unintended consequence of the fragmentation of procedural law in those countries, which after many years and commendable efforts in relation to codification, have succeeded in enacting general procedural

[224] Cadiet et al. 2010, pp. 142–178.

[225] Sobrie 2016, p. 46.; de Leval 2015, pp. 15–16.

[226] Rubenstein 2001–2002, pp. 1884–1885.

[227] Cfr. Zimmermann 2014, p. 21.

[228] Note that this tension is equally present in the United States. See Cover 1975, p. 718; Resnik 1982, p. 441.

laws precisely to replace the many previous procedures and reduce these to one common procedure".[229]

The warning may be too late as the process of fragmentation under the influence of EU law has already been going on for a while. Moreover, the Member States contribute themselves to this process by creating separate regimes in their legal orders for procedural law requirements originating in EU law. This is clearly visible in the Belgian legal order. Important parts of the procedural framework for damages actions in the context of competition law infringements have been laid down in the Code of Economic Law and not in the Judicial Code.[230] A special regime for the disclosure of evidence now exists outside the Judicial Code. Also, the judgment of the Antwerp Court of Appeal in *United Video Properties* has effectively created a different framework for the reimbursement of fees charged by party-appointed experts in the context of IP litigation. Similarly, the TSD may lead to a specific evidentiary regime for litigation involving trade secrets and the Court's case law regarding the UCTD requires a different relationship between judges and parties in the context of consumer law litigation, especially in default proceedings.

The issue of fragmentation could be overcome if the Member States would incorporate the sectoral EU law elements into a horizontal framework at national level. For example, the Belgian legislator could extend the solution for the reimbursement of fees charged by party-appointed experts under the IPED to the whole of civil litigation. Such solution would also prevent situations of reverse discrimination from arising.[231] The same goes for certain aspects of the PDD or the TSD, as well as for the case law of the Court of Justice regarding the *ex officio* application of the UCTD.

Fragmentation is thus not inevitable. It requires, however, a much bigger effort from the national legislator to insert a specific sectoral requirement in a horizontal framework. Moreover, it means that Member States will have to take over EU law solutions into their national framework. This raises, however, another crucial issue: who is responsible for the regulation of civil procedure in the European Union?

---

[229] Opinion of Advocate General Campos Sánchez-Bordona of 5 April 2016, *United Video Properties*, C-75/15, EU:C:2016:201, point 4.

[230] The same goes for, *inter alia*, Germany. The provisions of the PDD were implemented in the Law on Competition and not the Civil Procedure Code, including the regime for disclosure of evidence. See Gesetz gegen Wettbewerbsbeschränkungen in der Fassung der Bekanntmachung vom 26. Juni 2013 (BGBl. I S. 1750, 3245), das zuletzt durch Artikel 3 des Gesetzes vom 1. Juni 2017 (BGBl. I S. 1416) geändert worden ist, in particular § 33g. (To be consulted at http://www.gesetze-im-internet.de/gwb/BJNR252110998.html).

[231] Adinolfi 2012, pp. 287–288.

1.5.2 Competence for Regulation of Civil Procedure

When the EU's sectoral/functional approach to procedural law meets the horizontal/autonomous approach to procedural law of the Member States, two main options are possible in principle. On the one hand, a Member State may want to maintain a horizontal approach in order to resist fragmentation of civil procedure. This means that EU law requirements will have to be incorporated in a horizontal framework that applies to the whole of national civil procedure. In such a situation, Member States effectively give up regulatory powers in the field of civil procedure. On the other hand, a Member State may want to maintain regulatory powers, limiting the effects of EU law intervention in national procedural law to situations in which EU law applies. Constraining the regulatory impact of EU procedural rules will however lead to fragmentation of civil procedure. The choice for the Member States is thus between uniformity/loss of regulatory powers and fragmentation/retaining regulatory powers.

What option would be chosen by the Member States? I argue that Member States will in the end choose a uniform approach to civil procedure above maintaining powers to regulate civil procedure, especially in the long run.[232]

It is unlikely that Member States will give up easily the horizontal approach to civil procedure, which has prevailed for many years and is deeply entrenched in thinking about civil procedure.[233] It may thus be expected that the first option will prevail over the second option. This seems also the natural flow of things. When EU law requirements conflict with national civil procedure, the consequence is likely to play out as follows. First, the primacy of EU law has as a consequence that an EU law requirement will prevail over a rule of national civil procedure in a given conflict. Second, once the EU law requirement prevails over a national procedural rule that is part of a horizontal framework, it can be expected that the national preference for horizontality will extend the EU law solution to all cases regulated by that procedural rule. The horizontal approach at national level will thus cause the effect that the EU standard is being applied across the board, far beyond the scope of EU law. This way the Member States can maintain their policy to have a coherent and uniform civil procedural law. It means, however, that the content of such horizontal framework will be to a large extent determined by EU law. This is also what can be expected in regard of the Belgian legal framework for the reimbursement party-appointed expert fees, given the legislator's penchant for a horizontal approach.

The other option, maintaining regulatory freedom by compromising on uniformity is less likely to occur, certainly in the long run. At first, it may be envisaged

[232] It may of course not be excluded that for certain specific situations a specific solution may be maintained. The overall approach will, however, go in the direction of maintaining uniformity and conceding regulatory powers.

[233] See, for example, Cadiet 2006, pp. 7–8; Laenens et al. 2016, pp. 18–19.

that Member States maintain minimal exceptions to uniformity.[234] For example, Belgium has provided for an exceptional disclosure regime in the context of damages actions for violations of competition law. Further to this, an exceptional regime currently exists as well for the reimbursement of costs for legal assistance by experts in the field of IP litigation. The limited nature of these exceptions may be a convincing reason for the legislator to compromise on uniformity in favour of regulatory freedom. The question is what may happen in the long run. If the EU continues to lay down rules or requirements that lead to the creation of various exceptional regimes in national civil procedure, it means that it also progressively limits the regulatory freedom of the Member States. When this goes on, a tipping point may be reached after which both uniformity and regulatory freedom are severely affected. It may then no longer be preferable to maintain exceptional regimes because the trade-off will be less interesting, with EU law providing special procedural regimes for an increasing number of substantive law areas. This would imply a double loss for the Member States, affecting both the uniformity of procedural law and the regulatory powers of the Member States.

Member States will then have to make a new choice. Under the current model, limiting the impact of EU law on national civil procedure would imply limiting the EU's powers to regulate substantive law issues.[235] Thus, unless the Member States would decide to revoke a large amount of powers from the EU (or exit or wind down the EU), it is very unlikely that the EU will cease to exercise influence over national civil procedure. Quite to the contrary.[236] It may then be expected that Member States will attempt to secure the horizontality of civil procedure by incorporating EU sectoral rules in a horizontal framework.[237] This will lead to a situation in which EU law lays down the standard for national civil procedure, with Member States using the discretion allotted to them to turn sectoral rules into common rules.[238]

1.5.3 The Future of Civil Procedure Regulation in the EU

The process sketched above implies that the effects of specific EU rules on civil procedure in particular substantive law contexts may in the long run lead to a harmonisation of standards of civil procedure throughout the Member States. This

[234] See Conant 2002, p. 32.

[235] Cfr. Miquel Sala 2008, p. 214.

[236] Wagner 2008, p. 31.

[237] Cfr. Krans 2010, p. 164.

[238] Cfr. Wagner 2008, p. 18: "Diese Materialisierung rechtsvergleichend zu informieren und normativ zu begleiten sowie die Fragmentierung des Zivilprozess- und Insolvenzrechts zu einem Flickenteppich von Sondermaterien zu verhindern – dies wird eine der Kernaufgaben der kommenden Jahre sein".

is due to the spill-over effects of EU law legislation and the case law of the Court.[239] The principle of conferral is not able to contain the ramifications of a valid exercise of EU competences. It is a typical phenomenon that can also be witnessed in other areas of law where national law is influenced by EU law requirements.[240] It is equally a reminder of the fact that civil procedure is not a unique area of national law deserving of a special doctrine shielding it from EU law influence.

That being said, this does not mean that Member States will lose their regulatory powers completely. They will continue to exercise them, but at the level of the EU in the Council of the European Union.

1.6 Concluding Remarks

This contribution briefly considers the impact of EU law on national civil procedure. The Belgian situation was taken as a point of departure to highlight a number of evolutions and as a basis for further reflection. The considerations regarding the fragmentation of civil procedure and the increasing influence of the EU over the regulatory powers of the Member States in the area of civil procedure transcend, however, the Belgian legal order.

These evolutions pose a number of fundamental questions regarding the regulation of civil procedure and the conceptualisation of procedural law across the European Union. This warrants a principled approach and deserves a proper reflection. However, choices are currently being made incidentally, mostly by the Court of Justice. This is unfortunate, given the fact that these choices have a transformative effect on the civil justice systems of the EU Member States.[241]

It is also noteworthy that this evolution, despite its importance, is not being met with proper reflection in the academic debate. Admittedly, many aspects of civil procedure have currently not yet been affected by EU law.[242] There is, however, an increasing impact that will continue to progress and expand to aspects of civil procedure that have remained unaffected at present. EU law is now part and parcel of our civil procedural laws and cannot be left out of the discussion. With this contribution I hope to have made a convincing argument for a more in-depth study of this highly interesting and important aspect of civil procedure. After all, it will be

---

239 McEldowney 2017, pp. 129–130; Craig 2015, pp. 289–290.

240 See, for example, regarding competition law: Opinion of Advocate General Kokott of 13 July 2006, *Confederación Española de Empresarios de Estaciones de Servicio*, C-217/05, EU:C:2006:473, paras 17–31.

241 Miquel Sala 2008, p. 217.

242 Wilman 2015, p. 512.

the task of national procedural lawyers to transform EU sectoral rules into a common procedural framework at national level, "ramener la diversité à l'unité en traduisant en principes généraux de demain les règles spéciales d'aujourd'hui".[243]

References

Adinolfi A (2012) The "procedural autonomy" of Member States and the constraints stemming from the ECJ's case law: Is judicial activism still necessary. In: Micklitz H-W, De Witte B (eds) The European Court of Justice and the autonomy of the Member States. Intersentia, Antwerp/Cambridge, pp 281–303

Bobek M (2012) Why there is no principle of "procedural autonomy" of the Member States. In: Micklitz H-W, De Witte B (eds) The European Court of Justice and the autonomy of the Member States. Intersentia, Antwerp/Cambridge, pp 305–323

Cadiet L (2006) Ouverture – D'un code à l'autre: de fondations en refondation. In: Cadiet L, Canivet G (eds) De la commémoration d'un code à l'autre: 200 ans de procédure civile en France. LexisNexis, Paris, pp 3–17

Chadelat C (2006) Point de vue – L'élaboration d'un code de procédure civile, entre pratique judiciaire et droit savant. In: Cadiet L, Canivet G (eds) De la commémoration d'un code à l'autre: 200 ans de procédure civile en France. LexisNexis, Paris, pp 48–74

Conant L (2002) Justice contained: Law and politics in the European Union. Cornell University Press, London/Ithaca

Cover RM (1975) For James Wm. Moore: Some reflections on a reading of the Rules. Yale Law Journal 84:718–740

Craig P (2015) UK, EU and global administrative law: Foundations and challenges. CUP, Cambridge

de Leval G (2015) Introduction. In: de Leval, Georges F (eds) Manuel de procédure civile. Larcier, Brussels

De Temmeran B (2003) De verhaalbaarheid van kosten van juridische of technische bijstand, Tijdschrift voor Privaatrecht 40:1013–1070

Dupont R (2016) La Directive relative à la protection des secrets d'affaires: quelques perspectives au regard du droit belge. Intellectuele Rechten/Droits intellectuels 2:150–157

Galetta D-U (2010) Procedural Autonomy of EU Member States: Paradise Lost? Springer, Berlin

Genn H (2010) Judging civil justice. Cambridge University Press, Cambridge

Gualco E, Lourenço L (2016) "Clash of Titans". General principles of EU law: Balancing and horizontal direct effect. European Papers 2:643–652

Haapaniemi P (2009) Procedural autonomy: A misnomer? In: Ervo L, Gräns M, Jokela A (eds) The Europeanization of procedural law and the new challenges to fair trial. Europa Law Publishing, Groningen/Amsterdam, pp 87–121

Halpérin J-L, Niboyet M-L (2014) Agir en justice: la distinction de la substance et de la procédure. In: Cadiet L, Dauchy S, Halpérin J-L (eds) Itinéraires d'histoire de la procédure civile. IRJS Editions, Paris, pp 5–27

Hess B (2010) Europäisches Zivilprozessrecht. C.F. Müller Verlag, Heidelberg

Jauering O, Hess B (2011) Zivilprozessrecht. C.H. Beck, München

Kakouris CM (1997) Do the Member States Possess Judicial Procedural "autonomy". CML Rev 34:1389–1412

Kilpatrick C (2001) Turning remedies around: A sectoral analysis of the Court of Justice. In: De Burca G, Weiler JHH (eds) The European Court of Justice. OUP, Oxford, pp 143–176

[243] Cadiet 2006, p. 16; Krans 2010, p. 163.

König J (2011) Der Äquivalenz- und Effektivitätsgrundsatz in der Rechtsprechnung der Europäischen Gerichtshofs. Nomos, Baden Baden
Kovar R (1973) L'effectivité interne du droit communautaire. In: Dehousse F (ed) La Communauté et ses états membres: Actes du sixième colloque de l'I.E.J.E. sur les Communautés européennes. Nijhoff, The Hague, pp 201–233
Krans B (2010) Nederlands burgerlijk procesrecht en materieel EU-recht. Kluwer, Deventer
Kroppenberg I, Linder N (2014) Coding the nation. Codification history from a (post-) global perspective. In: Duve T (ed) Entanglements in legal history: Conceptual approaches. Max Planck Institute for European Legal History, Frankfurt am Main, 67–99
Kulms K (2013) Der Effektivitätsgrundsatz. Nomos, Baden Baden
Laenens J, Broeckx K, Scheers D, Thiriar G (2016) Handboek gerechtelijk recht. Intersentia, Antwerpen/Cambridge
Le Baut-Ferrarese B (2010) CJCJ, 16 décembre 1976. In: Karpenschif M, Nourissat C (eds) Les grands arrêts de la jurisprudence de l'Union européenne. Thémis, Paris, pp 75–82
Lenaerts K, Maselis I, Gutman K, Nowak JT (2014) EU Procedural Law. Oxford University Press, Oxford
Loughlin M (2013) Why sovereignty? In: Rawlings R, Leyland P, Young A (eds) Sovereignty and the law. Oxford University Press, Oxford, pp 34–49
McEldowney J (2017) The Factortame litigation: Sovereignty in question. In: Juss S, Sunkin M (eds) Landmark cases in public law. Hart/Bloomsbury, Oxford/London, pp 115–141
Miquel Sala R (2008) European private law without European law on civil procedure? In: Vaquer A (eds) European Private Law Beyond the Common Frame of Reference. Europa Law Publishing, Groningen/Amsterdam
Mosselmans S (2016–2017) Taak van de rechter bij verstek. Rechtskundig Weekblad 1:3–24
Mosselmans S, Broeckx K, Taelman P (2016–2017) Geen blinde inwilligingsverplichting voor de rechter bij verstek. Rechtskundig Weekblad 28:1091–1095
Normand J (2006) Clôture. In: Cadiet L, Canivet G (eds) De la commémoration d'un code à l'autre: 200 ans de procédure civile en France. LexisNexis, Paris, pp 377–383
Półtorak N (2015) European Union rights in national courts. Kluwer Law International, Alphen aan den Rijn
Reich N (2014) General principles of EU civil law. Intersentia, Antwerp/Cambridge
Resnik J (1982) Managerial judges. Harvard Law Review 96:374–448
Rideau J (1972) Le rôle des Etats membres dans l'application du droit communautaire. Annuaire français du droit international 18:864–903
Rödl F (2015) Gerechtigkeit unter freien Gleichen. Eine normative Rekonstruktion von Delikt, Eigentum und Vertrag. Nomos, Baden Baden
Rubenstein W (2001–2002) The concept of equality in civil procedure. Cardozo Law Review 23:1865-1915
Scheers D, Thiriar P (2017–2018) Burgerlijk procesrecht na Potpourri V. Rechtskundig Weekblad 19: 723–734
Schermers H, Waelbroeck D (2001) Judicial protection in the European Union. Kluwer Law International, The Hague/London/New York
Schütze R (2015) European Union Law. Cambridge University Press, Cambridge
Sobrie S (2016) Procederen qualitate qua. Intersentia, Antwerp/Cambridge
Steennot R (2016) Strafsancties impliceren op zich geen absolute nietigheid. Journal des Juges de Paix 9:429-431
Steennot R (2017) De bescherming van de consument door het Hof van Justitie: een brug te ver? Tijdschrift voor Privaatrecht 54:81–180
Tack S (2005) Verhaalbaarheid verdedigingskosten. Nieuw Juridisch Weekblad 131:1298–1306
Van Caenegem R (1992) An historical introduction to private law. Cambridge University Press, Cambridge
Van Caenegem R (2002) European law in the past and the future. Cambridge University Press, Cambridge
Van Drooghenbroeck J-F (2016a) Le Code judiciaire en pot-pourri. Larcier, Brussels

Van Drooghenbroeck J-F (2016b) Réajustement de la protection du justiciable défaillant. In: Van Drooghenbroeck J-F (ed) Le Code judiciaire en pot-pourri. Larcier, Brussels, pp 197–249

Van Drooghenbroeck J-F, De Coninck B (2008) La loi du 21 avril 2007 sur la répétibilité des frais et honoraires d'avocat. Journal des Tribunaux pp 37–60

Van Gerven W (2000) Of rights, remedies and procedures. Common Market Law Review 37:501–536

Van Orshoven P (2016) Uitleiding. In: Allemeersch B, Taelman P (eds) De hervorming van de burgerlijke rechtspleging door Potpourri I. Die Keure, Bruges

Wagner G (2008) Entwicklungstendenzen und Forschungsperspektiven im Zivilprozess- und Insolvenzrecht. ZEuP 2008 1:6–31

Walker N (2013) Sovereignty frames and sovereignty claims. In: Rawlings R, Leyland P, Young A (eds) Sovereignty and the law. Oxford University Press, Oxford, pp 18–33

Wieacker F (1974) Industriegesellschaft und Privatrechtsordnung. Fischer Athenäum Taschenbücher Rechtswissenschaft, Frankfurt am Main

Wijffels A (2008) The Code de procedure civile (1806) in France, Belgium and the Netherlands. In: van Rhee CH, Heirbaut D, Storme M (eds) The French Code of civil procedure (1806) after 200 years. Kluwer, Mechelen, pp 5–73

Wilman F (2015) Private enforcement of EU law before national courts: The EU legislative framework. Edward Elgar, Cheltenham

Woolf H (1996) Access to Justice: Final report to the Lord Chancellor on the civil justice system in England and Wales. HMSO, London

Zekoll J (2006) Comparative Civil Procedure. In: Reimann M, Zimmermann R (eds) The Oxford Handbook of Comparative Law. Oxford University Press, Oxford, pp 1328–1362

Zimmermann R (2003) The civil law in European Codes. In: MacQueen HL, Vaquer A, Espiau Espiau S (eds) Regional private laws and codification in Europe. Cambridge University Press, Cambridge, pp 18–59

Zimmermann R (2014) Codification: The Civilian Experience Reconsidered on the Eve of a Common European Sales Law. In: Wang W-Y (eds) Codification in international perspective. Springer, Heidelberg, pp 11–43

Chapter 2
The Internationalisation of Procedural Law: The Law on Execution and Attachment Orders

Ton Jongbloed

Contents

Abstract Although much attention is paid to the European law of civil procedure, this mainly concerns the proceedings. An important catalyst is the criterion of Article 6 ECHR against which proceedings are compared. Proceedings must take place before an independent tribunal and must be concluded within a reasonable time. The fundamental principles of the law of civil procedure must also be met, such as hearing of both sides. Plans for harmonised European procedural law focus mainly on partial projects such as unification of time limits. But it will be clear that the enforcement of court decisions is of great significance. A person who obtains a judgment allowing his claim, but does not have possibilities to have the judgment

An extended version of the present contribution entitled 'Yes we can (in the near Future); the internationalisation of the Law of Execution and Attachment' has been published in: Koster et al. 2017, pp. 117–144.

T. Jongbloed (✉)
Law of Enforcement and Seizure, Molengraaff Institute for Private Law,
Utrecht University, Utrecht, The Netherlands
e-mail: a.w.jongbloed@uu.nl

V. Lazić and S. Stuij (eds.), *International Dispute Resolution*,
Short Studies in Private International Law,
https://doi.org/10.1007/978-94-6265-252-1_2

enforced will have won a Pyrrhic victory. There is a need for provisions on execution and attachment law in a European context. Our society is acquiring more and more of an international character. Some Dutch people think about buying a second home in France, Greece, Italy or Spain. But what can one do if the seller ultimately does not want to cooperate? What needs to happen if someone wants to buy a painting on location and pays the purchase price but the supplier does not want to surrender the painting? In such cases it is advisable that the same legal measures can be taken in the various EU countries, for example that attachment for the purpose of delivery can be imposed.

Keywords Attachment Orders · CEPEJ · Council of Europe · Harmonisation of European Procedural Law · Internationalisation of Procedural Law · Law of Execution and Seizure

2.1 Introduction

In a time in which full use was initially made of fax machines and is now being made of e-mails and WhatsApp messages and in which commercial trips are thought of in order to spend some time in space, saying that the world seems to have become 'smaller' is labouring an obvious point. Anyone who compares the procedural law in 2017 with that of half a century or one or two centuries ago discovers that legislation sometimes lags behind (legal) practice.

Viewed from a Dutch perspective, a lot has changed. Membership of the European Union and the Council of Europe has made many changes to procedural law, and the law of the countries surrounding us is no longer really 'foreign' to us anymore. After the (then still) European Economic Community (EEC) had finally realised that the free movement of persons, services and capital should be followed by the free movement of judgments, the Brussels Convention was concluded—the Convention on jurisdiction and the recognition and enforcement of judgments in civil and commercial matters of 1968.[1] On the one hand, this removed the inner borders so that a German defendant could not be summoned in the Netherlands pursuant to Section 126 subsection 3 of the previous Code of Civil Procedure (hereinafter: CCP), but had to be summoned before a court of his domicile in Germany. On the other hand, judgments and authentic instruments from the EC Member States were recognised in principle in other Member States so that after a judgment would be rendered in a Member State, renewed proceedings were no longer required to arrive at enforcement in another Member State. This is now the Regulation Brussels Ibis, applicable in all 28 Member States.[2] On the other hand,

[1] Cf. Verschuur 1995.

[2] Regulation (EU) No. 1215/2012 of the European Parliament and of the Council of 12 December 2012 on jurisdiction and the recognition and enforcement of judgments in civil and commercial matters, OJEU 2012 L351/1. See also Hazelhorst 2017.

the Convention for the Protection of Human Rights and Fundamental Freedoms from 1950 (ECHR), and particularly Article 6 relating to the right to a fair trial within a reasonable time by an independent and impartial tribunal, has harmonised a great deal of procedural legislation.[3]

2.2 The Need for Internationalisation in The Netherlands and Particularly Europeanisation Within the European Union

The Netherlands is a small country dealing with many foreign countries. The Netherlands is also a trading country: a major part of Dutch income comes from trade, import and export. In such a case a few conditions need to be met. Fixed exchange rates are a prerequisite, legal certainty is as well. As far as the latter is concerned, it should be clear how proceedings will run, what costs can be incurred in them, the extent to which the judiciary is independent, etc. The point is that the law in another State should be predictable and preferably resemble the law in one's own country as closely as possible.

First of all, of course, the sphere of application of Regulation Brussels Ibis had to be determined: to what countries and to what types of matters will the Regulation apply. Furthermore it should be clear which court has absolute and territorial jurisdiction and whether a domicile or a nationality criterion applies. But it also needs to be delineated when a judgment or authentic instrument qualifies for recognition and enforcement in another Member State. Recognition can also follow automatically—as if it were a domestic judgment—but one can also think of an exequatur procedure in which it is reviewed whether the principles of due process have been fulfilled[4] and ensured that there is no conflict with public order. Which documents must be submitted in such a case? A copy of an authentic judgment and/or a certificate? Is it to be submitted in the original language of the proceedings or in a translation? If the latter is the case, does it have to be translated into the language of the Member State of the enforcement or does a translation into one of the modern languages suffice? Is enforcement possible at all if another legal remedy can be used? To what extent can the jurisdiction of the foreign court be reviewed, certainly

---

[3] Cf. Section 20 subsection 1 CCP: The judge must guard against unreasonable delay of the proceedings and, if necessary, take measures at the request of a party or ex officio. The provision was included as a result of e.g. ECHR June 1987, *NJ (Dutch Law Reports) 1990, 231; ECLI:NL:XX:1987:AC9931*, Capuano/Italia (more about this below).

[4] Refusal to recognise a judgment is logical if the document initiating the proceedings has not been served in such a timely manner and in such a way on the respondent as was necessary with a view to his defence (unless the respondent has not used any legal remedies against the judgment while he was able to do so) or if the judgment is not compatible with an earlier judgment given between the same parties in a dispute over the same matter and based on the same cause, provided the earlier judgment meets the conditions for recognition in the requested Member State.

if the impression exists that jurisdiction has erroneously been established? Can that be done ex officio or must it be based on a request of a party? These are all questions that need to be answered when a recognition and/or enforcement of a foreign judgment is requested.

Once these answers have been given, a party to the proceedings can then assess how proceedings in a foreign country will run, such as, which requirements are set and which costs are likely to be incurred. In that way procedural law becomes predictable to a great(er) extent and a party to the proceedings will know that he/she will not be confronted with a 'black hole' that constantly results in new surprises. As will become evident below, harmonisation in a European context is the most logical. Naturally it would be best if regulations could be drafted that apply to (almost) all countries in the world. But that is not a realistic starting point. The legal cultures differ too much to make that possible at all times.

Examples can of course be given of instruments which very many countries have adopted. In that context one can immediately think of the Hague Conference on Private International Law (HCCH).[5] Within the framework of the Hague Conference, inter alia, the Procedural Law Convention 1954 was drafted: the Convention of 1 March 1954 on civil procedure, which replaces the Convention of 17 July 1905 on civil procedure. Also, the following conventions can be mentioned: Convention of 15 November 1965 on the Service Abroad of Judicial and Extrajudicial Documents in Civil or Commercial Matters, Convention of 1 February 1971 on the Recognition and Enforcement of Foreign Judgments in Civil and Commercial Matters, Convention of 18 March 1970 on the Taking of Evidence Abroad in Civil or Commercial Matters and the Convention of 2 October 1973 on the Recognition and Enforcement of Decisions Relating to Maintenance Obligations. This does not affect the fact that drafting sometimes runs with difficulty, the number of ratifications is disappointing or the differences are so great that they cannot be bridged.[6]

All things considered, it is not surprising that when harmonisation is thought of in the Netherlands, first of all a unification within the European Union comes to

[5] https://www.hcch.net. An intergovernmental organisation with the object of unifying the regulations of private international law. 81 states and the European Union are members of the Hague Conference. In addition, there are many observers, such as the Union Internationale de Huissiers de Justice (UIHJ) referred to below; http://www.uihj.com.

[6] From https://www.hcch.net/en/projects/legislative-projects/judgments I have taken: The "Judgments Project" refers to the work undertaken by the Hague Conference since 1992 on two key aspects of private international law in cross-border litigation in civil and commercial matters: the international jurisdiction of courts and the recognition and enforcement of their judgments abroad. Initially, the Judgments Project focussed on developing a broad convention, which was subsequently scaled down to focus on international cases involving choice of court agreements. This led to the conclusion of the Hague Convention of 30 June 2005 on Choice of Court Agreements ("Choice of Court Convention"). Work has been done for some time on the project Recognition and Enforcement of Foreign Civil Protection Orders.

mind. This may not always be a guarantee of success. Sometimes harmonisation in a specific case nevertheless goes too far. Besides, sometimes there are national procedures that work so well that there is no or hardly any need for a harmonised international procedure. Denmark is an example of the first type. Although it is a member of the European Union it has made a reservation to the regulations relating to judicial cooperation in civil and commercial matters. They are de facto declared inapplicable.[7] Other examples are the European Account Preservation Regulation (EAPO)[8] and the Regulation on Wills and Succession[9] which, unlike other judicial regulations, will not be applicable in the United Kingdom and Denmark. Examples of the second type are the European Order for Payment (EOP) Procedure and the European Small Claims Procedure (ESCP), mainly because the sphere of application was limited to no more than €2,000. The intention is to raise the competency level to €5,000.[10] Whether this will have much effect must be awaited, as much more attention is paid in the Netherlands to the drastic Quality and Innovation (Kei) legislation[11] and both regulations are 'on the radar' of (very) few lawyers.

---

[7] An exception was made for the Regulations Brussels I, Brussels Ibis and the Regulation on the Service of Documents. Denmark was already a party to the preceding 1968 Brussels Convention and the Regulation Brussels I has a certain added value. To prevent a convention from being concluded or the old one from having to be supplemented, Denmark ultimately subjected itself to the effect of this regulation.

[8] European Account Preservation Order. Cf. Regulation (EU) No. 655/2014 of 15 May 2014 establishing a European Account Preservation Order procedure to facilitate cross-border debt recovery in civil and commercial matters, OJEU 2014, L 189/59, as well as the Act of 14 November 2016, implementing Regulation (EU) No. 655/2014 of the European Parliament and of the Council of 15 May 2014 establishing a European Account Preservation Order procedure to facilitate cross-border debt recovery in civil and commercial matters (OJEU 27 June 2014, L 189) (Act Implementing the Regulation establishing a European Account Preservation Order procedure), Bulletin of Acts and Decrees (*Stb.*) 2016, 440.

[9] Regulation (EU) No 650/2012 of the European Parliament and of the Council of 4 July 2012 on jurisdiction, applicable law, recognition and enforcement of decisions and acceptance and enforcement of authentic instruments in matters of succession and on the creation of a European Certificate of Succession (OJEU of 27 July 2017, L 201/107).

[10] Act of 22 March 2017, Bulletin of Acts and Decrees 2017, 125, amending the Act implementing the European Regulation setting up a European Small Claims Procedure (ESCP) and the Act implementing the Regulation creating a European Order for Payment procedure and implementing Regulation (EU) 2015/2421 of the European Parliament and of the Council of 16 December 2015 amending Regulation (EC) No 861/2007 establishing a European Small Claims Procedure and implementing Regulation (EC) No. 1896/2006 creating a European order for payment procedure (OJEU 2015, L 341/1).

[11] Act of 13 July 2016, Bulletin of Acts and Decrees 2016, 288, amending the Dutch Code of Civil Procedure and the Dutch General Administrative Law Act in connection with the simplification and digitisation of procedural law.

Cf. Ahsmann 2015, pp. 65–66; Asser et al. 2015; Klaassen 2016, pp. 74–84; Rutten 2016, pp. 23–28 and Steenberghe and den Tonkelaar 2017.

2.3 The Importance of the Council of Europe and CEPEJ

Besides the European Union, another organisation plays a role not to be underestimated in the harmonisation of the law of civil procedure in Europe. This is the Council of Europe.[12] Unification is pursued there from a socio-cultural perspective, and not from an economic perspective. There are 47 countries which are members of the organisation and besides the 28 countries of the European Union, one can also think of Russia and Turkey. Undoubtedly the most familiar scheme is the Convention for the Protection of Human Rights and Fundamental Freedoms (ECHR) from 1950 and in relation to procedural law especially because of Article 6 (1) regarding the right to a fair trial:

> In the determination of his civil rights and obligations (…) everyone is entitled to a fair and public hearing within a reasonable time by an independent and impartial tribunal established by law. Judgment shall be pronounced publicly (…).

The article was 'rediscovered' around 1975 and afterwards the provision has influenced various decisions and judgments within the whole of procedural law.[13] I would like to point to the decisions *Airey/Ireland*, *Capuano/Italy*, *Hauschildt/Denmark* and *Goodwin*.[14]

A special commission within the Council of Europe also plays an important role in relation to harmonisation. This is the CEPEJ:[15] the European Commission for the Efficiency of Justice.[16] The creation of the CEPEJ demonstrates the will of the Council of Europe to promote the Rule of Law and Fundamental Rights in Europe, on the basis of the European Convention on Human Rights, and especially its Articles 5 (Right to liberty and security), 6 (Right to a fair trial), 13 (Right to an effective remedy) and 14 (Prohibition of discrimination). The establishment of CEPEJ is ensured by the Directorate General of Human Rights and Legal Affairs. It

---

[12] http://www.coe.int.

[13] See e.g. Smits 2008; Chébti 2015, pp. 1057–1061 and Hammerstein 2004, pp. 220–233.

[14] In Airey/Ireland (ECHR 9 October 1979, NJ 1980/376; ECLI:NL:XX:1979:AC1044 it is made clear that the right to `access to the court' should have a practical meaning and that financial obstacles should not prevent this. In Capuano/Italy (ECHR 25 June 1987, NJ 1990/231; ECLI:NL:XX:1987:AC9931) it was ruled that the State is liable if and in so far as the judge can be blamed if proceedings last unnecessarily long. The impartiality of the judge has an objective and a subjective component, as is evident from Hauschildt/Denmark (ECHR 24 May 1989, NJ 1990/627; ECLI:NL:XX:1989:AD0800), Dombo (ECHR 27 October 1993, NJ 1994/534; ECLI:NL:XX:1993:AD1977) shows that the principle of equal treatment is violated if statements by parties to the proceedings are given different value, depending on who bears the burden of proof (in that case there is additional evidentiary value pursuant to Section 164 subsection 2 CCP and otherwise non-binding evidentiary value pursuant to Section 152 subsection 2 CCP), while in Goodwin (ECHR 27 March 1996, NJ 1996/577; ECLI:NL:XX:1996:AD2519) journalistic privilege is recognised.

[15] Commission européenne pour l'efficacité de la justice; Cf. http://www.coe.int/cepej.

[16] This commission was established on 18 September 2002 by Resolution Res (2002)12 of the Committee of Ministers of the Council of Europe.

shows the intention of the Council of Europe not only to elaborate on international legal instruments, but also to promote a precise knowledge of the judicial systems in Europe.

The CEPEJ will have, among other duties, the task of continuing the on-going reflexion about the potential offered by new information technologies (IT) to improve the efficiency of justice. The functioning of the CEPEJ is governed by its Statute (cf. Appendix 2 to Resolution Res (2002)12).

The aim of the CEPEJ is the improvement of the efficiency and functioning of justice in the member States, and the development of the implementation of the instruments adopted by the Council of Europe to this end.

Its tasks are:

- to analyse the results of the judicial systems;
- to identify the difficulties they meet;
- to define concrete ways to improve, on the one hand, the evaluation of their results, and, on the other hand, the functioning of these systems;
- to provide assistance to member States, at their request;
- to propose to the competent authorities of the Council of Europe the fields where it would be desirable to elaborate a new legal instrument.

In order to carry out these different tasks, the CEPEJ prepares benchmarks, collects and analyses data, defines instruments and means of evaluation, adopts documents (reports, advices, guidelines, action plans), develops contacts with qualified personalities, non-governmental organisations, research institutes and information centres, organises hearings, promotes networks of legal professionals.

Reports are published on a regular basis in which the different countries are compared and from which the governments can learn. In the series European judicial systems, efficiency and quality of justice, the 2016 CEPEJ study 23 Edition 2016 (2014 data)[17] was published in 2016 and as study 24 a Thematic report: Use of information technology in European courts. In this way the possibility is offered to learn from best practices and a finger is kept on the pulse: no country wants to be at the bottom of a list showing for example that the costs of proceedings there are the highest or the procedures last the longest.

---

[17] In this numerous subjects are compared, such as Budgets of judicial systems (Annual budget of the whole justice system, Annual public budget of the judicial system, Budget allocated to courts, Annual public budget allocated to the public prosecution services, Court taxes or fees, Annual public budget allocated to legal aid and Trends and conclusions), Judicial staff and lawyers (Judges, Prosecutors, Other staff in courts and Lawyers), Court organisation and court users (Organisation of the court system, Quality of the court system and court users and Monitoring of the violations of ECHR Article 6) and Efficiency and quality of the activity of courts and public prosecutors (General overview of court workload, Civil and commercial justice (litigious cases), Administrative justice, Criminal justice, and Trends and conclusions).

2.4 An Area Suitable for Unification: Execution and Attachment Law

Although much attention is paid to the European law of civil procedure, this mainly concerns the proceedings.[18] An important catalyst is the criterion of Article 6 ECHR against which proceedings are compared. Proceedings must take place before an independent tribunal and must be concluded within a reasonable time. The fundamental principles of the law of civil procedure must also be met, such as hearing of both sides. Plans for harmonised European procedural law focus mainly on partial projects such as unification of time limits. But it will be clear that the enforcement of court decisions is of great significance. A person who obtains a judgment allowing his claim, but does not have possibilities to have the judgment enforced will have won a Pyrrhic victory.

The necessary steps have meanwhile been taken. Particularly the Regulation Brussels Ibis is of great importance. Another example from 18 January 2017 is the Regulation on the European Account Preservation Order (EAPO),[19] but this offers Dutch creditors few possibilities and the application of Dutch law (giving creditors much more possibilities to ensure their claim) will often be preferred.[20]

As a rule, however, attention is focused on questions such as which court has jurisdiction to proceed, how are the proceedings carried out, what to do if the summoned person fails to enter the appearance and which legal remedies are available. Relatively little attention is paid to the possibility and manner of enforcement. This is expressed in education,[21] the activities of CEPEJ on this level and in the case law of the Luxembourg Court of Justice (CJEU) and the Strasbourg

[18] It is worthwhile to mention Article 81 of the Treaty on the functioning of the European Union: The Union shall develop judicial cooperation in civil matters having cross-border implications, based on the principle of mutual recognition of judgments and of decisions in extrajudicial cases. Such cooperation may include the adoption of measures for the approximation of the laws and regulations of the Member States.

In §2 it is said that measures shall be adopted, particularly when necessary for the proper functioning of the internal market. Eight specific measures are mentioned.

Furthermore article 47 of the Charter of Fundamental Rights of the European Union also gives a right to an effective remedy and to a fair trial.

[19] European Account Preservation Order. Cf. Regulation (EU) No. 655/2014 of 15 May 2014 establishing a European Account Preservation Order procedure to facilitate cross-border recovery of debts in civil and commercial matters, OJEU 2014, L 189/59.

[20] See Jongbloed 2014, pp. 20–31. At the time this text was concluded, not a single EAPO seizure had yet been imposed in the Netherlands.

[21] For instance, from 2017, the Utrecht bachelor students have only been taught a limited number of areas in the law of civil and administrative procedure, and this does not include the enforcement of court judgments. Those who graduate in private law still encounter this component in the Civil Litigation Practice course, but a person who graduates in administrative or criminal law is not taught execution and attachment law. The courses for private law students have often be halved as well, as until a few years ago, an optional course existed that taught this area of law for eight weeks, whereas the course now lasts only four weeks.

Court of Human Rights (ECHR). It should be noted first of all that although the Council of Europe or CEPEJ has undertaken activities, this was done quite some time ago. For example, Recommendation Rec (2003)17 of the Committee of Ministers to Member States on enforcement[22] was adopted in 2003 and the Guidelines for a better implementation of the existing Council of Europe's

[22] https://search.coe.int/cm/Pages/result_details.aspx?ObjectID=09000016805df135.

The main points from the Recommendation from 2003 are:

III.1 In order for enforcement procedures to be as effective and efficient as possible,

a. enforcement should be defined and underpinned by a clear legal framework, setting out the powers, rights and responsibilities of the parties and third parties;

b. enforcement should be carried out in compliance with the relevant law and judicial decisions. Any legislation should be sufficiently detailed to provide legal certainty and transparency to the process, as well as to provide for this process to be as foreseeable and efficient as possible;

c. the parties should have a duty to co-operate appropriately in the enforcement process; in addition, and particularly in family law matters, the relevant authorities should facilitate this co-operation;

d. defendants should provide up-to-date information on their income, assets and on other relevant matters;

e. states should set up a mechanism to prevent misuse of the enforcement process by either party which should not be considered as a re-adjudication of the case;

f. there should be no postponement of the enforcement process unless there are reasons prescribed by law. Postponement may be subject to review by the court;

g. during the enforcement process, a proper balance should be struck between claimants' and defendants' interests, bearing in mind, in particular, the provisions of both Articles 6 and 8 of the ECHR. Where appropriate, the interests of third parties should also be taken into account. When the enforcement process concerns family law matters, the interests of the members of the family should be taken into account; in addition, when the enforcement process concerns, in particular, the rights of children, the best interests of the child should be a primary consideration, in accordance with international and national law;

h. certain essential assets and income of the defendant should be protected, such as basic household goods, basic social allowances, monies for essential medical needs and necessary working tools.

III.2 Enforcement procedures should:

a. be clearly defined and easy for enforcement agents to administer;

b. prescribe an exhaustive definition and listing of enforceable titles and how they become effective;

c. clearly define the rights and duties of defendants, claimants and third parties, including, in the two latter cases, their rankings and entitlements to monies recovered and distributed amongst claimants;

d. provide for the most effective and appropriate means of serving documents (for example, personal service by enforcement agents, electronic means, post);

e. provide for measures to deter or prevent procedural abuses;

f. prescribe a right for parties to request the suspension of the enforcement in order to ensure the protection of their rights and interests;

g. prescribe, where appropriate, a right of review of judicial and non-judicial decisions made during the enforcement process.

III.3 Enforcement fees should be reasonable, prescribed by law and made known in advance to the parties.

recommendation on enforcement[23] in December 2009. The last activity is the first and only Global Forum on Enforcement which was organised by CEPEJ and UIHJ on 10 December 2014.[24]

One of the first important judgments of the ECHR is the *Silva Pontes* case.[25] This case concerns a man who was involved in a serious traffic accident on 12 November 1975. His car collided with a car from the firm of Dos Reis. He sustained serious injuries in the accident, as a result of which he remained partially incapable of work in spite of various operations. On 20 December 1977 Silva Pontes brought a civil action against, among others, Dos Reis and the latter's firm for compensation of the loss sustained. Compensation was requested also for the loss yet to be sustained as a result of the accident in an amount to be determined partly in the execution proceedings. The claim was allowed on 1 October 1982 as far as the loss sustained was concerned. On 13 October 1982 he brought an appeal concerning the level of the amount awarded. After this was dismissed on 30 May 1985, he submitted a request to the High Court of Justice on 11 July 1985, which on 5 February 1987 awarded an amount to be determined in the execution proceedings for loss as a result of permanent invalidity and incapacity for work. On 28 October 1987, he started execution proceedings which were settled out of court on 19 December 1989. Meanwhile, 14 years had passed and the question was whether a reasonable period existed within the meaning of Article 6 ECHR. Concisely stated, the ECtHR ruled that the reasonable time in civil proceedings pursuant to Article 6 ECHR also includes the follow-up proceedings for the determination of damages and the execution proceedings. This means that in execution proceedings, a judge must indeed take account of the progress of the preceding stages of the proceedings, even if they took place before a different court.

Hornsby/Greece[26] is another case which is constantly referred to. This case concerned a judgment ordering the Greek state to undertake certain measures. However, in the five years after the judgment had been rendered, no measures had yet been taken to implement that judgment:

> 40 The Court reiterates that, according to its established case-law, Article 6 § 1 secures to everyone the right to have any claim relating to his civil rights and obligations brought before a court or tribunal; in this way it embodies the 'right to a court', of which the right of access, that is the right to institute proceedings before courts in civil matters, constitutes one aspect (see the Philis v. Greece (no. 1) judgment of 27 August 1991, Series A no. 209, p. 20, § 59). However, that right would be illusory if a Contracting State's domestic legal system allowed a final, binding judicial decision to remain inoperative to the detriment of one party. It would be inconceivable that Article 6 should describe in detail procedural

---

[23] https://wcd.coe.int/ViewDoc.jsp?p=&Ref=CEPEJ(2009)11&Language=lanEnglish&Ver=original&BackColorInternet=eff2fa&BackColorIntranet=eff2fa&BackColorLogged=c1cbe6&direct=true.

[24] http://www.coe.int/t/dghl/cooperation/cepej/meetings/2014/Forum_Enforcement/Dossier_special_Forum_Enforcement_2014_en.asp.

[25] ECHR 23 March 1994, NJ 1994/506; ECLI:NL:XX:1994:AD2065 (*Silva Pontes*).

[26] ECHR 19 March 1997, NJ 1998/434; ECLI:NL:XX:1997:AD2709 (*Hornsby v. Greece*).

guarantees afforded to litigants — proceedings that are fair, public and expeditious — without protecting the implementation of judicial decisions; to construe Article 6 as being concerned exclusively with access to a court and the conduct of proceedings would be likely to lead to situations incompatible with the principle of the rule of law which the Contracting States undertook to respect when they ratified the Convention (see, mutatis mutandis, the Golder v. the United Kingdom judgment of 7 May 1974, Series A no. 18, pp. 16–18, § 34–36. Execution of a judgment given by any court must therefore be regarded as an integral part of the 'trial' for the purposes of Article 6; moreover, the Court has already accepted this principle in cases concerning the length of proceedings (see, most recently, the Di Pede v. Italy and Zappia v. Italy judgments of 26 September 1996, Reports of Judgments and Decisions— 1996, pp.…, §§ …).'

An important judgment of the CJEU is *Capelloni v. Pelkmans.*[27] Pelkmans had obtained leave on 19 December 1980 from the *Corte d'appello* in Brescia (Italy) to enforce the judgment of the Breda District Court of 8 May 2015, ordering Capelloni to pay Pelkmans a sum of money. Capelloni lodged objection pursuant to Article 36 of the Brussels Convention, also at the *Corte d'appello* in Brescia. But before a decision had been taken on the objection, Pelkmans imposed prejudgment attachment pursuant to Article 39 of the Brussels Convention on immovable property belonging to Capelloni. Pelkmans subsequently requested the *Corte d'appello* to validate this attachment in accordance with Section 680 of the Italian Code of Civil Procedure. After the *Corte d'appello* had declared Pelkmans' application inadmissible, the Italian *Corte Suprema di Cassazione*, in a decision of 9 November 1983, applied to the CJEU for a preliminary ruling on the interpretation of Article 39 Brussels Convention: To what extent must the provisions in the different national legal systems be referred to for similar measures in order to adopt the rules governing the protective measures in Article 39.[28] The CJEU (Fourth Chamber) ruled as follows:[29]

(1) 'By virtue of Article 39 of the Convention, a party who has applied for and obtained authorization for enforcement may, within the period mentioned in that article, proceed directly with protective measures against the property of the party against whom enforcement is sought and under no obligation to obtain specific authorization.
(2) A party who has obtained authorization for enforcement may proceed with the protective measures referred to in Article 39 until the expiry of the period prescribed in Article 36 for lodging an appeal and, if such an appeal is lodged, until a decision is given thereon.

[27] CJEU 3 October 1985, NJ 1987/118; ECLI:EU:C:1985:388 (*Capelloni v. Pelkmans*).

[28] Under Italian law, authorisation was required from the competent court for each prejudgment attachment, so the interested party could not immediately proceed to impose attachment; prejudgment attachment had to be imposed within a peremptory period that started on the day on which the interested party was able to impose attachment, and after the attachment was imposed, validation proceedings had to be instituted.

[29] See present Articles 39 (enforcement) and 46 ff. (refusal of enforcement) Brussels Ibis.

(3) A party who has proceeded with the protective measures referred to in Article 39 of the Convention is under no obligation to obtain, in respect of those measures, any confirmatory judgment required by the national law of the court in question.'

The second decision to be mentioned is *Mund v. Hatrex.*[30] In that judgment it was decided that Article 7 of the EEC Treaty in conjunction with Article 220 of the EEC Treaty and the 1968 Brussels Convention preclude application of a national provision of the law of civil procedure which in the event of a judgment to be enforced on its own national territory allows prejudgment attachment only on the ground that without such a measure enforcement would probably be impossible or considerably more difficult, while it already allows such attachment in the event of a judgment to be enforced in another Member State, merely on the ground that the judgment will have to be enforced abroad. A Member State may make a difference between domestic situations and cases in which facts are connected with other Member States, but there must be justification for doing so. But because the 1968 Brussels Convention exists, there was no such justification. As the provisions in the German *Zivilprozessordnung* (ZPO) were in conflict with the prohibition on discrimination according to nationality in the EC Treaty, the provision had to remain inapplicable.

Although these are important judgments, all things considered the harvest is limited and the question arises whether further steps can be taken. I am of the opinion that this question must be answered in the affirmative. Because practice shows that a judgment for allowance is no reason to cheer. Sometimes an allowing judgment must be presented for review by an executing judge who must assess whether the judgment in question should or should not be enforced. The starting point at times is that the oldest judgment must be enforced first. A noble pursuit that, however, leads to problems in practice: if there is a backlog, it sometimes takes a few years before a judgment can be enforced and, in that case, it still remains to be seen whether the debtor has departed to an unknown destination (because not all countries have sound population records). A third complication could be that there are too few officials charged with enforcement. Finally, a complication can also occur if the rates are set at too high a level (for example on the transition to enforcement by bailiffs as officers under private law and no longer as officers under public law), because enforcement is then not possible in all cases. After all, if there is enforcement by private officers and not by public servants who are paid by the government, those who insist on enforcement will have to advance the costs of this and must then wait and see if those costs can be recovered from the debtor.

[30] CJEC 10 February 1994, NJ 1994/385; ECLI:EU:C:1994:52 (*Mund v. Hatrex*).

2.5 What To Do Next?

It is clear from the foregoing that there is a need for provisions on execution and attachment law in a European context. Our society is acquiring more and more of an international character. While Dutch people used to go on holiday to the Veluwe or Ardennes, it is now the most usual thing in the world to travel to countries such as Spain, Italy and Greece. Some people think about buying a second home in those countries. But what can one do if the seller ultimately does not want to cooperate? What needs to happen if someone wants to buy a painting on location and pays the purchase price but the supplier does not want to surrender the painting? In such cases it is advisable that the same legal measures can be taken in the various EU countries,[31] for example that attachment for the purpose of delivery can be imposed.

It can be pointed out that attachments can be subdivided. There are prejudgment attachments as opposed to executory attachments. Furthermore, there are attachments against a debtor, a third party or a creditor itself. Attachment is possible of movables, property subject to registration, aircraft, ships, bearer rights or rights by order and of shares, of rights under a capital sum policy or life insurance. Attachment can be for the purpose of recovery or surrender or delivery. And, an important point: there are indirect means of execution such as an incremental penalty and commitment for failure to comply with a judicial order, because it is not always possible by far to compel the agreed performance. For example, a stage actress who can sign a lucrative contract elsewhere and is no longer motivated to perform for her present employer. Such an employer cannot bring her to the theatre. But if someone is affected financially or if someone is temporarily deprived of his/her liberty by an unwanted stay in the House of Detention, it is often possible to achieve what was agreed.

Another obstacle is that law on attachment proves to be very diverse when recovery is sought. It is not surprising that goods intended for public service cannot be attached (Cf. Sections 436 and 703 of the Dutch CCP). But there are provisions in the different legal systems expressing that certain goods may not be attached. For example, under Section 475e there is an income tax allowance in the event of periodic payments.

On the one hand a creditor must have the possibility to seek recovery from the assets and income of the debtor,[32] but the legislature also realised that the debtor may/should not be plucked down to the bone. For instance, no attachment is possible of clothing, food and beverages for a month and tools that are necessary to acquire income. For instance, an income tax allowance applies to wages and other

---

[31] An obstacle is however that national purchasing law differs. In France, one already becomes the owner through the purchase, whereas in the Netherlands, transfer is still necessary. In order to revendicate ownership, it is much simpler if one has to take legal action on the basis of a personal right. This means that uniform purchasing law is a primary need.

[32] Cf. Book 3, Sections 276 and 296 of the Dutch Civil Code. The same in France as well: Section 2284 Code Civil.

income. In Dutch situations, the amount of income someone needs to leave free can be fixed on the basis of the standard of living applicable in the Netherlands: the incomes that roughly equal 90% of the statutory assistance criterion cannot be attached and the debtor can use them to pay rent or mortgage interest, food and beverages, heating of the home etc. But if a debtor living in a foreign country is involved, the standard of living there has to be considered and it would not be simple for a Dutch court to determine the right amount.

Moreover, it is possible that the debtor hardly earns any income in the Netherlands, or has income that remains below the statutory assistance criterion, but has considerable income in the country of residence. It is, however, difficult to find out if there is such income and what is the amount. An unfair situation could occur if the income in the Netherlands is less than the statutory assistance criterion, but the foreign income exceeds it. All this was a reason at the time for the legislature to grant persons living abroad a protected earnings level in principle if the court awards this on their application.[33] In such a case the court can deliver 'customised work'.

If non-attachable movables are concerned, a Dutch creditor can be over-optimistic, but have a rude awakening. It appears in fact that in most countries of Europe, the group of items of property that cannot be attached is much larger than in the Netherlands.

I already pointed this out in 2002.[34] Further research in relation to the preliminary advice of the Royal Dutch Organization of Bailiffs (KBvG) published in 2012 confirmed that.[35] The Dutch scheme proves in fact still to be the scheme from 1838. No attachment can be imposed on clothing, food and beverages for a month and tools that are needed to acquire income. Two possibilities have been dropped, namely first of all that no attachment can be imposed on the equipment of persons in military service. In addition, the possibility has disappeared from the law that no attachment can be imposed on a cow, or two pigs, or two goats, or four sheep, at the discretion of the person against whom attachment is made, with the necessary hay and feed for that livestock for a month. No exceptions have been added, however. This is remarkable, because in other countries the legislature has sought to be in line with the increased social welfare, which has resulted in legislative amendments that extended attachment.

In many countries a choice appears to have been made to leave a debtor in possession of what are viewed nowadays as essential necessities of life. Think of the movables needed for the subsistence and work of the attached person and his family, as well as the items of property that are indispensable for disabled persons or the care of the sick. In addition, sometimes attachment cannot be imposed on

---

[33] Cf. *Kamerstukken (Parliamentary Papers) II* 1982/83, 17 897, General scheme for garnishment of wages, social benefits and other periodic payments, No. 3, Explanatory Memorandum, pp. 11 and 20.'

[34] Cf. pp. 50–53 and pp. 59–65 of my oration. I already argued at the time in favour of extending the scheme and adjusting it to the countries surrounding us.

[35] Cf. Rijsdijk and Nijenhuis 2012.

items of property a testator or donor has declared not capable of attachment. The doctrine of abuse of rights also proves to play a role. The starting point of the right of recovery is (still) that a creditor can recover from all items of property of his debtor (Section 276 Book 3 of the Dutch Civil Code ('Burgerlijk Wetboek', or '*BW*'))[36] and that the creditor may exercise this right in respect of all items of property at the same time. He is, after all, at liberty to impose attachment on all items of property capable of attachment (Section 435 subsection 1 CCP). But those main rules can be derogated from if a greater interest is served than that of the individual creditor in recovering his debt.

In many countries the law contains a more extensive list and attachment is not possible, for example[37] of computers in use by children of school age, the household items that are needed to preserve, prepare and consume food, the table and chairs to consume meals together, a wardrobe and store cupboard. But also household effects such as a sewing machine, bicycle, clock, vacuum cleaner, radio and television set, a refrigerator, a washing machine and a tumble dryer. Strictly personal items such as photographs, letters and awards also fall outside the reach of the attaching party. The same holds de facto for pets such as cats and dogs.[38] In Section 1412ter of the Belgian Judicial Code ('*Gerechtelijk Wetboek*'), a scheme is included relating to cultural property owned by a foreign power that is located in Belgium for exhibition purposes. It appears to me that this scheme of non-attachable property could be harmonised in a relatively simple way by formulating an open standard that gives bailiffs the freedom to act as they see fit within a limit to be set by the European Commission. The European Commission could be inspired by the 'non-excessiveness criterion' referred to in Section 295 subsection 4 under 4 of the Bankruptcy Act ('Faillissementswet', or '*Fw*') that in applies in our country in the context of the Act on debt repayment of natural persons ('*Wet schuldsanering natuurlijke personen', or* '*Wsnp*'), but could also choose an amount derived for example from the minimum income in a country. The situation can be assessed from case to case, taking account of the circumstances of the case. I expect that the bailiff handling the matter (and if necessary also the judge, who can always be asked for an opinion) will also be inspired by the list existing at present, but that 'firm' standards formulated in the law will be prevented from resulting in cases of unfairness.

In this way, a reasonable balance could be found between, on the one hand, the principle that the debtor warrants his debts with his entire assets and, on the other, the principle on which the debt management scheme is based that a debtor must be offered the opportunity to work on a solution for his debts so that he can participate fully in social life again.

---

[36] Also in France: Cf. Section 2284 Code Civil.

[37] For Belgium see Section 1408 Judicial Code; Germany § 811 in conjunction with 930 ZPO; France: Sec. 14 of the Act of 9 July 1991, no. 650 and for the United Kingdom Section 89 County Court Act 1984 and Scheme 7 under 9 subsection 3 to the Courts Act 2003.

[38] This too with a view to practical aspects such as care. If a pedigree cat or dog is concerned, attachment may indeed come up for discussion.

A similar solution could be found for the protected earnings level when it comes to periodic income.[39] The starting point could be a certain percentage of the minimum income or the statutory assistance criterion, with attention to several circumstances which are assessed as a flat-rate starting point. But a correction could be applied to this in order to do justice to the circumstances of the actual case. One has higher housing costs out of necessity than the other; one lives closer to his work and the other does not; one has growing children, the other does not. A bit tricky: one has a higher spending pattern than the other. By this I do not mean that, by definition, someone who spends a lot should be given a higher or lower protected earnings level. But some spend proportionately less on themselves and are able to pay off their debts more quickly. In fact, the solution referred to here is what judges already do in determining maintenance, namely doing justice within predetermined limits to the circumstances of the specific case. It would now be alleged against this that legal inequality would occur in that way because one person will be affected more and the other person less by the attachment. One can reply to this: this may be the case in absolute amounts, but the point is to arrive at a fair outcome. The person who receives a higher protected earnings level will have more costs and the surplus may go to the landlord or be spent on diet food. I think that justice can be done precisely by delivering custom work via a protected earnings level. I understand from bailiffs that they weigh the debtor with respect to his/her ability to pay and that it is often better to set a realistic amount that the debtor has left after deduction of a protected earnings level than that the debtor is 'squeezed' because the latter will lose the motivation to make efforts to pay off the debts as soon as possible. And two things should be borne in mind: 1. It is ultimately the judge who rules and 2. The problem does not need to be solved in 45 min; by exchanging ideas a properly operating system can be found.

Another question can be raised as well. Does such a system constitute discrimination because the residents of the various Member States are assessed differently? It is evident from the aforementioned judgment of the CJEU of 10 February 1994, *NJ* 1994, 385 (*Mund v. Hatrex*) that residents of the European Union must be treated equally. The court held in paragraph 14:[40]

> The Court has consistently held that this provision[41] prohibits any discrimination on grounds of nationality within the field of application of the Treaty. This article forbids not only overt forms of discrimination based on nationality, but also all covert forms of

[39] See also Rijsdijk et al. 2014.

[40] See also CJEC 29 October 1980, *NJ* 1981, 655; ECLI:EU:C:1980:251 (*Boussac v. GerstenMayer*), legal ground 9: 'Article 7 of the Treaty (now Article 12 of the EC Treaty, AWJ) prohibits any discrimination on grounds of nationality within the field of application of the Treaty. That article forbids not only overt discrimination by reason of nationality, but also all covert forms of discrimination which, by the application of other criteria of distinction, lead in fact to the same result.'

[41] Cf. present Articles 2 and 3 of the EU Treaty as well as Article 21 of the Charter of Fundamental Rights of the EU.

discrimination which, by the application of other criteria of differentiation, lead in fact to the same result.

This, however, concerns a prohibition of discrimination based on nationality. If the persons located on the territory of a Member State are treated equally and no other specific obstacles are raised, there is no question of this. The fact that the law in one Member State is not exactly the same as that in another Member State does not need to form a problem. If I should live on a farm in Romania, for example, no attachment could be imposed on part of my livestock (nor on the feed). In reverse, if a Spaniard is located in the Netherlands, garnishment of his wage would be limited to—briefly stated—90% of the Dutch statutory assistance criterion. Equal cases are then treated equally.

There are even parts that are easy to harmonise, and even unify. In that case I think of both coercive measures incremental penalty and commitment for failure to comply with a judicial order. It is not possible to compel a court judgment in all cases. More than 80 years ago—on 1 April 1933[42]—the Dutch legislature included the incremental penalty scheme in the Code of Civil Procedure. The incremental penalty is an additional order to pay the creditor a sum of money, without any connection to the loss the creditor is sustaining or will sustain as a result of late performance of the main obligation, in order to exert pressure on the debtor to comply with the main order pronounced against him. It is usually calculated per day of delay in implementing the order or per violation of the order.

The aim was that in this way less use needed to be made of the imposition of commitment for failure to comply with a judicial order and the hope was that hitting a debtor in his wallet would give him/her a substantial impetus to comply. Briefly stated, this comes down to obligations to give can indeed be compelled, whereas obligations to do or omit (not to do) have to fall back on incremental penalties or commitment for failure to comply with a judicial order. The incremental penalty has indeed been called the main procedural law innovation of the twentieth century.[43]

A Uniform Benelux Act on Incremental Penalty Payments has meanwhile been applied for almost 40 years in the Netherlands, Belgium and Luxembourg.[44] While Belgium abolished commitment for failure to comply with a judicial order on the introduction of the incremental penalty payment 1980, this institution was retained in the Netherlands. Although the number of cases in which commitment is imposed annually is limited, the institution nevertheless has a useful function. As a last resort, someone can be deprived of his liberty by transfer to the House of Detention. It can be said that the law shows its teeth in this way. The importance of commitment for failure to comply with a judicial order is illustrated on the basis of a

[42] Cf. the Act of 29 December 1932, *Bulletin of Acts and Decrees (Stb.)* 676.

[43] Quoted from Drion 1982, p. 126. The great importance of including the incremental penalty in the law also emerges from Scholten 1980, which states on pp. 317–319 that the introduction of the incremental penalty was the cause of a shift in the term 'obligation'.

[44] Cf. Jongbloed 1991, pp. 349–366 and Jongbloed 2003, pp. 193–255.

ruling by the President of the District Court of The Hague of 31 May 2012.[45] The husband had to pay partner maintenance after the divorce. After a change to the maintenance with retroactive effect, there were arrears of payment of almost €115 000. The wealthy father of the husband had died and the husband rejected the inheritance from his father. His daughters of majority age therefore took the husband's place as heirs. On the day of rejection, the husband concluded a contract with his daughters in which agreements were made in relation to the husband's rejection of the estate and its administration by his daughters of the share in the inheritance to which they were entitled. Briefly stated, the husband was nevertheless able to have considerable capital at his disposal by way of a joint account with one daughter and an interest-free loan with the other daughter. In this case, attachments for the purpose of recovery did not produce much. From September 2011 a sum of €10.35 a month was withheld from the husband's state pension benefit and from December 2011 a sum of €1006.10 a month from his benefit under the Victims of Persecution (1940–1945) Benefits Act ('*Wet uitkeringen vervolgingsslachtoffers 1940–1945*' or '*WUV*'). From the amounts withheld costs including those of the bailiff, were paid. On balance, since March 2012 the wife has received a sum of €950 gross per month. The attachment of the husband's dwelling had no effect because the value of the dwelling was estimated at €190,000 and the husband had two mortgage loans, one of €98,400 from Rabobank and one of €131,000 from his daughter. The attachment imposed on the husband's bank accounts did not have effect either. The Court was of the opinion that the husband provided insufficient insight into the capital at his disposal, and which he can actually can have at his disposal, and the total amount of the estate of the husband's father and the way in which it was divided is not sufficiently evident from the documents. It should be clear that this was not a case of inability to pay, but of unwillingness to pay. It will not be surprising that the wife's claim for commitment for failure to comply with a judicial order was allowed, and for a period of six months at most. If the husband did not pay, he could think in all peace and quiet in the House of Detention about what the future would entail for him. Because, for the sake of all clarity: the application of commitment for failure to comply with a judicial order does not cancel the obligation to pay the overdue partner maintenance.

So much experience has been gained with the scheme of the incremental penalty and commitment for failure to comply with a judicial order that it can simply be laid down in an EU Regulation. The Storme Commission published a report in 1994 entitled 'Approximation of Judiciary Law in the European Union',[46] which contained the building blocks for a harmonised law of civil procedure. The incremental penalty was one of those building blocks.

[45] District Court of The Hague, 31 May 2012, ECLI:NL:RBSGR:2012:BX7581.

[46] Storme 1994.

2.6 A Short-Term Solution

The Union Internationale des Huissiers de Justice (UIHJ) was already mentioned above.[47] An important objective of the UIHJ is to establish uniform regulations: the UIHJ board members travel all across the world to place their knowledge and experience at the service of governments and international organisations. In doing so, attention is paid first of all, on the one hand, to unification of the national laws of civil procedure and drafting treaties and conventions, but they emphasise as well that an independent 'officer of the court' is of great importance for the enforcement of judicial judgments/decisions.

Since 2008 the UIHJ has had a 'think tank' at their disposal in the form of a *conseil scientifique.* Its members are high court judges and university professors from all parts of the world.[48] Owing to their practical experience and knowledge of various legal systems, they constitute a good forum for drafting uniform regulations. The Tunisian Nadhir Ben Ammou is now Minister of Justice and Jacqueline Lohoues-Oble held that post for the Ivory Coast. The group gets together on a regular basis under the direction of Fricero and has drafted a Global Code of Enforcement in consultation with UIHJ president Andrieux.

The 'Global Code of Enforcement' project was given shape bit by bit. It was examined whether a draft rule was acceptable and reformulation often took place. A logical order also had to be set out. A choice was made for a subdivision into five parts. After the fundamental principles, attention was devoted to bailiffs and other persons charged with the enforcement of warrants of execution. The judicial authorities are mentioned in part 3, after which common provisions relating to enforcement measures and common provisions relating to preliminary measures follow.

It is no surprise that the fundamental principles were put first and foremost, as they are the core of the material to be regulated. Persons in possession of a warrant of execution had to be assured, for example, that there was an effective possibility for enforcement. It is in line with this that a debtor warrants his debts with his entire assets and can be compelled to make a statement of his possessions. Likewise, the costs of enforcement also have to be charged to the debtor, but the creditor must pay them in advance because otherwise the party charged with enforcement would not be certain of payment for his services and therefore might not want to take any action. Consequently, it was added that in case of insolvency of the debtor, the creditor will bear the costs. Should it be established that the right of execution has

---

[47] The UIHJ was established in 1952 by Belgium, France, Greece, Italy, Luxembourg, the Netherlands and Switzerland. Meanwhile, 86 countries have become members. http://www.uihj.com/en/.

[48] Cf. http://www.uihj.com/en/installation-of-the-scientific-council-of-the-uihj-in-paris-on-june-20th-2008_1017701.html. The members come from Argentina, (Kemelmajer de Carlucci), Germany (Hess), France (Ferrand en Fricero), the Netherlands (author hereof), Portugal (Meira Lourenco), Romania (Les), Russia (Yarkov) Thailand (Vattanahattai) and the US (Emerson).

been abused, the court can order the creditor to pay the costs of enforcement and compensate the debtor for the damage and/or loss sustained. It is also important for the costs of execution to be laid down, predictable, transparent and reasonable. On the other hand, the state must see to it that all information known about the place of residence, registered office or head office of the debtor, as well as the structure of the possessions is provided to the parties charged with enforcement.

An important point is to ensure that all creditors have equal access to the possibilities for enforcement, so that foreign or small creditors do not have to join at the back of the queue. It implies as well that states must give up their privileges. In virtually all countries it is made clear that enforcement can take place only at times determined by the legislature. Elaboration has been left to the national legislatures, because national circumstances play a part. We can think of national holidays and commemorative days, but also the time at which the sun rises and sets.

It is essential to bring the service of the warrant of execution to the debtor's attention prior to enforcement. Here, too, elaboration takes place in national law. This also opens the possibility to reach an amicable solution.

In practice a two-way split sometimes occurs between new technological resources and legislation that has not yet been adjusted to this. Consequently, it is stated that use can be made of new technologies in the hope that this will urge states to keep their legislation up to date.

Bailiffs can be impeded in performing their duties. Therefore, assistance should be guaranteed within a reasonable time of the professional persons charged with enforcing warrants of execution who request this. In line with that, in the context of effecting an executory measure, bailiffs must be able to enter the house and grounds of the debtor, even without the latter's permission or in the latter's absence. When the debtor's property is located at a third party, authorisation by the court is required for entry. Otherwise, the third parties right to inviolability of the home would be violated.

All measures with extraterritorial effect must be carried out by a bailiff of the state of the place of enforcement. This ensures a connection with the national legislation and decreases the chance of shortcomings.

Parts 2 and 3 centre on the officers charged with enforcement (in short: bailiffs) and the judicial authorities. Not just a random somebody may be charged with enforcement, but this must be someone who is specifically appointed in the national legislation, which ensures that competency requirements have been met. This concerns a ministerial duty and professional secrecy, but it is also stated that there must be *éducation permanente* and that rules must be laid down on professional ethics.

To monitor quality, disciplinary law is provided for that complies with the rules of a fair trial before an independent body that decides in proceedings where both sides are heard. In addition, disciplinary penalties must be in proportion to the gravity of the offences committed, and appeal must be possible against a disciplinary decision. Disciplinary law is also important in connection with the possibility to develop side activities. This will vary from country to country, but the starting point will be that bailiffs can be authorised to proceed with the amicable collection of debts.

Differences undoubtedly occur in enforcement. It is important that only a judge can rule on disputes arising from enforcement. Judges are considered to be independent and impartial and that cannot be said of all government officials, because the government is sometimes a stakeholder. Judges should also have the possibility to suspend or cancel enforcement.

The Code concludes in parts 4 and 5 with common provisions on enforcement and preliminary measures. It is stated first of all that all property can be attached unless it has been declared protected from attachment by national law. In the event of attachment of a bank account, an amount must be left at the debtor's disposal that is sufficient to maintain him and his family, the level of which is determined by law. Because the schemes differ on this point, the drafters sufficed with formulating a general starting point that must be specified by the national legislature. Clarity should also be observed regarding immunity: this should be clearly formulated in national legislation, particularly with respect to the state and public bodies, as well as with respect to diplomatic staff.

For the sake of certainty, a rule was formulated regarding the proportionality of enforcement measures: they must be in proportion to the amount of the claim. In case of abuse the creditor can be required to pay compensation. The same category of self-evident rules covers the autonomy of the bailiff: he applies the enforcement measure independently in a manner that prejudices the creditor's rights and the fundamental rights of the debtor as little as possible. States must, however, organise their enforcement systems in such a way that it is in line with the creditor's interests and the economic and social situation of the debtor. Consequently, a variety of execution measures should exist so that the bailiff can choose them according to the circumstances of the case.

Commitment for failure to comply with a judicial order, a radical coercive measure, exists in many countries. It is stated that its enforcement against persons must comply with international conventions, charters and declarations, as well as that imprisonment for civil-law debts is prohibited. It is fundamentally wrong to enforce it against family members of the debtor, while an eye must especially be kept on the interests of children.

Anyone in possession of a warrant of execution may proceed to enforce it. But for other cases a right to a provisional or protective measure must be included in the legislation, because otherwise it might not be possible to implement (alleged) rights.

The Global Code strikes a balance between the rights of the creditor on the one hand and, on the other, protection of the fundamental rights of the debtor. It is also special that there is insistence on the use of new methods and technologies to modernise the execution procedure. Not so long ago, a bailiff received an engagement to impose garnishment at a bank by e-mail, after which the bailiff brought the essentials in printed form to the attention of the bank, where the information was subsequently processed again in a digital file. This entailed unnecessary costs. In the future, there must be a connection with digital reality.

Should national legislatures observe the principles of the Global Code, harmonisation would be simple and possible in the short term, as the preliminary work has been done.

2.7 A Solution in the Longer Term

In the past, several Regulations and Directives were introduced in the law of the 28 EU Member States.[49] But we have to think of the future. What should be done?

There are four options:

1. Doing nothing at all.
2. Compilation and consolidation (maintaining the status quo, accompanied by setting out existing minimum standards in one instrument, possibly also of guidelines on application).
3. Comprehensive review, a 'Roadmap' and subsequent further legislation (where the Roadmap would contain the key principles, and further pieces of binding legislation would cover specific aspects or stages of civil procedure).
4. Creating a binding instrument containing minimum standards (adoption of a binding instrument containing common minimum standards (CMS), or a binding instrument containing common minimum standards (CMS) accompanied by a non-binding instrument concerning further, more detailed standards and some detailed rules as a suggested method of application of these standards in practice. Ultimately there should be an EU Code of Civil Procedure.

At present, the EU has limited legislative competence to regulate civil procedure: it relates to matters with cross-border implications. The fundamental limiting feature of Article 81 Treaty on the functioning of the European Union is that the EU has the power to only regulate 'matters with cross-border implications'.

For the existing EU legislation on civil procedure adopted on the basis of Article 81 'cross-border implications' entail a cross-border case: one with a cross-border element. But a more liberal interpretation is possible if we take into account the nature of the matters regulated (for example common minimum standards in civil procedure). Improving judicial cooperation, enhancing mutual trust, fairness of civil justice, and protection of fundamental rights can be regarded as having cross-border implications.

[49] E.g. European Enforcement Order, European Order for Payment, European Small Claims Procedure, Regulation (EU) No 1215/2012 on jurisdiction and the recognition and enforcement of judgments in civil and commercial matters, Regulation (EC) No 2201/2003 concerning jurisdiction and the recognition and enforcement of judgments in matrimonial matters and the matters of parental responsibility, Regulation (EC) No 1393/2007 on the service in the Member States of judicial and extrajudicial documents in civil or commercial matters (service of documents).

It is sometimes said that civil procedure rules are difficult to harmonise. Civil procedure is deeply enshrined in each nation's political organisation, social and economic structure, its constitutional and social identity, as well as arrangements for wealth distribution.

But I think a lot of people will welcome further harmonisation. And with the elimination of exequatur by the recast Brussels I Regulation, the issue of mutual trust comes to the fore and requires a common approach to the principle of a fair trial. This means that we need harmonisation of certain fundamental procedural principles and standards.

I think the existing differences in national civil procedure rules should not be overly exaggerated. We have common ground in the Napoleonic Code of Civil Procedure, Article 6 of the European Convention on Human Rights: the right to a fair trial, the right to have access to justice, Article 47 of the Charter of Fundamental Rights of the European Union and the CEPEJ reports.

We should probably do it the American way: procedural law in the United States of America varies from state to state. But American procedural law has already been largely harmonised by the introduction of the Federal Rules of Civil Procedure, which have also extensively influenced procedural law at the level of the separate States. I think this is what the Storme Commission had in mind. At that moment only a few politicians were interested in that idea, but nowadays a lot has been realised by regulations and directives. Times are changing and that could mean that procedural rules can be harmonised.

References

Ahsmann MJAM (2015) KEI: steengoed of drijfzand. Tijdschrift voor de Procespraktijk, pp 65–66

Asser WHD et al (2015) Procesinnovatie: KEIgoede ideeën. Procesrechtelijke reeks NVvP 32, Boom Juridische Uitgevers, Den Haag

Chébti M (2015) Misbruik van procesrecht door advocaten, rechterlijke terughoudendheid en het recht op toegang tot de rechter gewaarborgd in art. 6 EVRM. WPNR 2015/7087, pp 1057–1061

Drion H (1982) Geschriften van H. Drion. Kluwer, Deventer, pp 97–126

Hammerstein A (2004) De invloed van art. 6 EVRM op het burgerlijk procesrecht. In: Corstens GJM et al (eds) Europeanisering van het Nederlands recht; opstellen aangeboden aan mr. W.E. Haak. Kluwer Deventer, pp 220–233

Hazelhorst MI (2017) Free Movement of Civil Judgments in the European Union and the Right to a Fair Trial. T.M.C. Asser Press, The Hague

Jongbloed AW (1991) De dwangsom in Nederland, België en Luxemburg. In: Kokkini-Iatridou D, Grosheide FW (ed) Molengrafica. Eenvormig en vergelijkend privaatrecht 1991. Vermande, Lelystad, pp 349–366

Jongbloed AW (2003) De dwangsom als een speciale sanctie in het Europese privaatrecht. In: Storme M (ed) Procedural Laws in Europe; Towards Harmonisation. Maklu, Antwerpen/Apeldoorn, pp 193–255

Jongbloed AW (2014) European seizure of bank accounts, but then different. Beslag en Executie in de Rechtspraktijk 2014, no. 5, pp 20–31

Klaassen CJM (2016) De civiele procedure volgens 'KEI'. RM Themis, pp 74–84

Koster H et al (2017) Essays on Private and Business Law (A Tribute to Professor Adriaan Dorresteijn). Eleven International Publishing, The Hague

Rijsdijk J, Nijenhuis J (eds) (2012) Herziening van het beslagverbod roerende zaken, een achterhaalde regeling bij de tijd gebracht. Preliminary advice of the Royal Dutch Organization of Bailiffs (KBvG). SDU, The Hague

Rijsdijk J et al (eds) (2014) Naar een nieuwe beslagvrije voet; Vereenvoudiging in een tweetrapsraket. Preliminary advice by the Royal Dutch Organisation of Bailiffs (KBvG). SDU, The Hague

Rutten JH (2016) KEI voor de gerechtsdeurwaarderspraktijk; De nieuwe procedure onder KEI in eerste aanleg. De Gerechtsdeurwaarder 2016/2, pp 23–28

Scholten GJ (1980) De invloed van wijzigingen in het procesrecht op het burgerlijk recht. WPNR 1980-5517, pp 317–321

Smits P (2008) Artikel 6 EVRM en de civiele procedure. Serie Burgerlijk Proces & Praktijk 10. Kluwer, Deventer

Steenberghe HMM, den Tonkelaar JDA (eds) (2017) Commentaar & Context KEI; het gewijzigde Wetboek van Burgerlijke Rechtsvordering becommentarieerd vanuit de parlementaire geschiedenis van de KEI-wetgeving. Boom juridische uitgevers, The Hague

Storme M (ed) (1994) Rapprochement du Droit Judiciaire de l'Union européenne – Approximation of Judiciary Law in the European Union. Kluwer Law International, Dordrecht

Verschuur RCh (1995) Vrij verkeer van vonnissen. Diss. Utrecht, Kluwer, Deventer

Chapter 3
Harmonisation of Conflict of Law Rules in the US? The Example of Recognition and Enforcement of Foreign Money Judgments

Elsemiek Apers

Contents

Elsemiek Apers is a legal advisor for the International Council of the Belgian Notariat, Bergstraat 30–32, 1000 Brussels, Belgium. elsemiek.apers@fednot.be. This chapter has been written in a private capacity.

E. Apers (✉)
International Council of the Belgian Notariat, Bergstraat 30–32, 1000, Brussels, Belgium
e-mail: elsemiek.apers@fednot.be

V. Lazić and S. Stuij (eds.), *International Dispute Resolution*,
Short Studies in Private International Law,
https://doi.org/10.1007/978-94-6265-252-1_3

Abstract Where the EU has experienced a wave of harmonisation—Europeanisation—of private international law rules, the same cannot be said for the US. This chapter, which uses recognition and enforcement of foreign money judgments as an example, shows that 'Americanisation' of private international law rules is not high on the agenda of the federal legislator. The basis for the law on recognition and enforcement in the US can be found in a case from 1895 and has since developed along the lines of non-binding model Acts, drafted by scholarly organisations. Although most US states have adopted legislation inspired by such model rules and Acts, others still adhere to common law principles, leaving the US with a non-harmonised, non-uniform regime. The latest attempt at harmonisation is a proposed statute of the American Law Institute, dating back to 2005, which has received as a main critique that it proposes a reciprocity condition. Yet, scholars do agree that actual harmonisation of the rules on recognition and enforcement of money judgments in the US will only be beneficial for businesses, private individuals and the country as a whole.

Keywords Conflict of laws · Recognition · Enforcement · Harmonisation · United States · American Law Institute

3.1 Introduction

The volume of trade between the US and the EU is, to say the least, considerable: around US $270 billion of export leaving the US and US $416 billion of imports into the US in 2016 alone.[1] Next to an economic component, trade also leads to legal relationships. Those relationships are governed by a vast number of contracts, most of which will—hopefully—contain clauses on private international law,[2] be it via arbitration or not. In addition to agreements between private parties, international agreements and national laws will contain rules on jurisdiction, applicable law and recognition and enforcement of judgments to guide parties in case of international disputes that may arise in the course of commerce. Furthermore, international family relationships also give rise to international disputes. After parties find themselves before a competent court and the applicable law has been determined, the question arises how the 'winning' party can find proper recourse for a judgment in a foreign state. This is especially important where the debtor of the judgment is located outside of the US and does not comply with the judgment, which in turn is relevant in the context of the recognition and enforcement of judgments. The examination of the private international law rules, and for the purposes of this chapter, the rules on recognition and enforcement, in a more globalised world is therefore an important issue.

[1] https://www.census.gov/foreign-trade/balance/c0003.html. Accessed on 12 December 2017.

[2] In the US, the term 'conflict of laws' is mostly used: this term, however, more literally only refers to a conflict in applicable law, whereas this chapter will focus on recognition and enforcement. Therefore, the term 'private international law' will be used.

This chapter explores the degree to which, if at all, the rules on recognition and enforcement of foreign money judgments in the US are harmonised. As the US remains a common law system, the differences with the codified rules on recognition and enforcement in the EU seem to be significant at first glance. Rules on recognition and enforcement form the cornerstone of EU private international law and the facilitation of free movement by means of near to automatic procedures is one of the main goals of the European Commission.[3] The same cannot be said for the US. Providing codified rules for recognition and enforcement is not high on the list of priorities for US lawmakers, nor is the conclusion of bilateral or multilateral agreements between states a pressing matter.[4]

Therefore, we will find a somewhat fragmented landscape, with both state and federal rules, but without a comprehensive unified set of rules to follow.[5] Indeed, as this chapter concludes later on, there is no harmonisation of rules on recognition and enforcement of foreign judgments in the US by way of a uniform law. However, there might be other ways to come to the same or similar result via alternative means and those will be explored below.

It must be noted here as well that the US is comprised of two different systems when it comes to recognition and enforcement, depending on whether the judgment comes from another US state, or from outside of the US. Judgments coming from sister-states can enjoy the treatment of the so-called Full Faith and Credit Clause from the US Constitution.[6] This clause provides that a judgment from a US state will be recognised and enforced by the other states.[7] This chapter however will focus on money judgments coming from outside the US, which will be referred to as 'foreign' judgments. Where necessary, reference will be made to 'sister state' judgments.

[3] The rules on recognition and enforcement formed part of the Brussels Convention, the first private international law instrument that was drafted by the six members of what would later become the European Union. See in general Dickinson 2015, pp. 1–10; Magnus 2016, pp. 10–23.

[4] A rare example that confirms the standard here is 'The Agreement between the Netherlands and the United States for the enforcement of maintenance (support) obligations' (Netherlands Treaty Series 2001, 117 and 134), which entered into force in May 2002. Also, the Hague Convention on Choice of Court Agreements contains clauses on recognition and enforcement of judgments rendered on the basis of an exclusive choice of forum agreement.

[5] Brand 2013, p. 494.

[6] US Constitution Article IV, para 1: "Full Faith and Credit shall be given in each State to public acts, records, and judicial proceedings of every other Sate". Little 2013, pp. 833–840.

[7] Schmitt 2013, p. 487. For a general discussion of this clause, see Sachs 2009, pp. 1201–1279.

3.2 The Basis of Recognition and Enforcement of Foreign Judgments in the US

3.2.1 *Preliminary Remarks*

Before getting into the details of the current rules on recognition and enforcement, it is important to outline the context and the historic developments that have led to the present rules, even more so since the US follows a common law tradition. Before the US gained its independence in 1776, law was primarily formed through case law. It was only since the end of the 19th century that more statutes were enacted, yet it has taken quite a while before private international law rules were provided for in statutory law. The US legal system can be characterised as a hybrid system of statutory law and common law developed through both the court systems and judicial interpretation of case law and statutes.

Where in the EU von Savigny was a very influential scholar who has shaped the private international law field, in the US Joseph Story fulfilled a seminal role and was inspired by Ulrich Huber and his idea of comity.[8] In principle, Story found that when a foreign court has proper jurisdiction, the judgment has to be recognised in other jurisdictions: this idea of comity has embedded itself in US conflict of laws.[9]

3.2.2 *Federal v. State Law*

A very important feature which has shaped the development of rules on recognition and enforcement in the past, is the division between the federal and state level. This distinction, and the case law concerning it, laid the foundations for the major principles in this area of law.

The US Constitution gives the federal government a certain, and limited, amount of powers.[10] The US Supreme Court, through early case law, has added to these powers a form of 'implied' powers, which are, according to the Court, necessary to effectively carry out the powers laid down in the Constitution.[11] Recognition and enforcement of foreign judgments as such are not powers given to the federal government and the doctrine of implied powers has up to today not been used to bring it under federal control.[12] Therefore, the US still has 50 different systems for the recognition and enforcement of foreign judgments. As will be shown below,

[8] Singal 2008, pp. 948–949.

[9] Story 1834, p. 492.

[10] US Constitution Article I.

[11] Rosner 2004, p. 325.

[12] As early as in 1926, the New York Court of Appeals found it to be a state issue, in *Johnson v Compagnie Generale Transatlantique* 242 N.Y. 381,152 N.E 121, 123 (1926).

most states in practice have adopted statutes on the matter that are to a certain extent similar.

Also, the US knows two parallel court systems. Both on federal and state level there is a trial court, an appeals court and a court of last resort.[13] At the state level each state has a supreme court, at federal level there are 13 appellate courts and the US Supreme Court sits in Washington D.C.[14] Two main cases, *Hilton* and *Erie*, have influenced the coming into existence of a recognition regime in the US. Before *Hilton*, foreign judgments were not given any conclusive effect and had to be tried again before a US court.[15]

3.2.2.1 *Hilton v Guyot*: The Basis for Recognition of Foreign Judgments

The first landmark case described here, *Hilton v. Guyot*, changed the view on conclusive effect.[16] The case dates back to 1895 and concerns a French judgment which awards Guyot, with domicile in France, a sum of money to be paid by Hilton, who was domiciled in the US. Mr. Guyot brought the French judgment to a New York circuit court, where he brought a suit requesting leave for enforcement. The court granted this, but Hilton appealed. The case went all the way to the US Supreme Court, where the argument was raised that foreign judgements are not enforceable in US courts.[17]

The Court used federal common law to decide the case and acknowledged that no statutes or treaties existed on the matter. It was of the opinion that both previous decisions and works of other legal experts led to the conclusion that foreign judgments cannot bear any more effect than prima facie evidence. Then however, the Court brought its argument based on the principle of comity and held that this was not a matter of absolute obligation, yet neither a mere courtesy.[18] The interpretation of comity in this case meant that recognition should also carry with it conclusive effects, when certain conditions were met: (1) the foreign court had proper jurisdiction to hear the case; (2) it provided a full and fair trial (due process); (3) the judgment did not conflict with public policy; (4) the judgment was not the result of fraud.[19] These four requirements are still the core of recognition and enforcement in the US today.

After an extensive comparative review, the Court deduced a fifth requirement, that of reciprocity. It found that this requirement was present in many legal systems,

[13] Burnham 2011, p. 167.

[14] Burnham 2011, p. 173. See in general www.uscourts.gov.

[15] This followed the English case law at the time, see Rosner 2004, p. 327.

[16] *Hilton v. Guyot* 159 US 113 (1895).

[17] In cases where the parties were not citizens of the same State, the federal courts had jurisdiction.

[18] Weston 2011, p. 738.

[19] *Hilton v. Guyot* at 202–203.

and a necessary component for granting foreign judgments conclusive effects in the US.[20] Ironically enough, France did not seem to provide reciprocity and thus Guyot could not benefit from the new standard the Court had just set: recognition was denied. The reciprocity requirement is still present in the statutes of some states, but has been abolished by most others.[21]

3.2.2.2 *Erie R. Co. v. Tompkins*

The fact that the US Supreme Court used federal common law in a case in which codified federal law does not exist, has led to criticism in later case law.[22] The matter was finally settled in another landmark decision from 1938, *Erie*.[23] The facts of this case did not pertain to private international law, and it was about more than just the question on which law should apply. Most important for this chapter however is the doctrine emanating from *Erie*, namely that when a federal court is presented with a state law question—in this case related to the recognition and enforcement of a judgment—it shall apply the law of the state in which it sits. The case law departed from what was previously decided in *Hilton*, where principles of federal common law were used.[24] It has thus been confirmed by the Supreme Court as early as 1938, that the US knows 50 different state-level systems for recognition and enforcement of judgments. The line of reasoning set out in *Erie* was later on confirmed in a case which did concern an issue of private international law, *Klaxon*.[25] Here, a New York based corporation sued a Delaware based corporation for breach of contract in a federal district court in Delaware. After winning the case, the New York corporation also asked for interest to be added to the sum of money already awarded, based on a New York Civil Procedure Act. This was granted by the Delaware court which was of the opinion that New York law applied, without consideration of the law of Delaware. The Supreme Court did not agree with this view and held that a federal court should apply the conflict of laws rules from the state in which it sits. In this case, the conflict of laws rules of Delaware.

[20] Ibid., at 227.

[21] See for example *Somportex Ltd. v Phila. Chewing Gum Corp.*, 453 F.2d 435, 440 n.8 (3d Cir. 1971), cert. denied, 405 U.S. 1017 (1972).

[22] See *Johnson v Compagnie Générale Transatlantique* 242 N.Y. 381, 152 N.E. 121 (1926).

[23] *Erie R. Co. v Tompkins* 304 U.S 64 (1938).

[24] The use of federal common law principles had been established even before *Hilton*, in a case stemming from 1842, see *Swift v Tyson* 41 U.S (16 Pet.) 865 (1842).

[25] *Klaxon Co. v Stentor Electric Mfg. Co.* 313 U.S. 487 (1941).

3.3 The 1962 and 2005 Acts and the Third Restatement: An Attempt at Harmonisation?

3.3.1 Preliminary Remarks

It is clear that courts hearing a case for recognition will apply state law. The question then remains what that state law might comprise, in the absence of any federal regulation. There are several sources and each state has either enacted statutes or follows principles of common law. Furthermore, there is both state and federal case law to draw from. A form of the comity approach as developed in *Hilton* is used by all states, be it via enacted legislation or through common law. If there is no statute or case law available, it is not easy to predict the outcome of the case, as the court relies on common law principles or draws from out-of-state precedents.[26] Very few states have in practice upheld the reciprocity requirement as an additional condition.[27] In this paragraph the relevant content of, and relationship between, the most commonly used instruments of recognition and enforcement will be discussed.[28]

3.3.2 The 1962 Uniform Foreign Money-Judgments Recognition Act

In 1962, the Uniform Law Commission drafted a first act on recognition of foreign money judgments, the Uniform Foreign Money-Judgments Recognition Act (UFMJRA).[29] The ULC is a non-profit organisation which has as its goal to "*provide states with non-partisan, well-conceived and well-drafted legislation that brings clarity and stability to critical areas of state statutory law*".[30] The acts are of a non-binding nature, yet they are an authoritative source for states when enacting binding legislation. Before the 2005 Act—discussed below—was drafted, 32 states had adopted statutes corresponding with or at least similar to the 1962 Act. The Act

[26] Rosner 2004, p. 336.

[27] Florida, North Carolina, Maine, Georgia, Ohio, Idaho, Massachusetts, and Texas.

[28] For a table containing an overview of the 1962 Act, the 2005 Act and the 2005 ALI proposed statute, see Brand 2013, pp. 536–537.

[29] To be found at http://www.uniformlaws.org/shared/docs/foreign%20money%20judgments%20recognition/ufmjra%20final%20act.pdf.

[30] Also called the National Conference of Commissioners on Uniform State Laws. As can be found on their website, www.uniformlaws.org, it is a non-profit organisation, founded in 1892, made up of practicing lawyers, judges, legislators, legislative staff and law professors appointed by state governments as commissioners.

itself is short, containing only 11 sections and without clear provisions on the burden of proof or on the actual procedure for enforcement.[31]

3.3.2.1 Principles for Recognition Under the 1962 UFMJRA

For the states which adhere to the 1962 Act, the basic principles are laid down in Sections 1 and 2. The foreign judgment must be final, conclusive, and enforceable in the state of origin. Judgments concerning taxes, fines and other penalties and judgments in matrimonial or family matters are excluded. When these conditions are met and none of the refusal grounds in Section 4 apply, the judgment must be recognised and the judgment has conclusive effect, pursuant to 3.

The 1962 Act does not contain a reciprocity requirement as put forward in *Hilton*. The Committee drafting the Act was of the opinion that many civil law countries did not recognise US judgments because foreign courts were unsure as to whether their local judgments would be recognised in the US.[32] The argument is that codification of the rules on recognition and enforcement by the different states would provide the clarity necessary for foreign courts to have more faith in the US recognition system, which in turn would lead foreign courts to be more willing to recognise US judgments.[33]

3.3.2.2 Refusal Grounds Under the 1962 UFMJRA

Section 4 provides the grounds upon which recognition must or may be refused. There are three mandatory grounds for refusal: (1) the foreign judgment was rendered under a system which does not provide for impartial tribunals or did not respect due process requirements; (2) the foreign court did not have personal jurisdiction; (3) the foreign court did not have subject matter jurisdiction.[34] Concerning the due process requirement, the comment provided by the Committee holds that a "*mere difference in the procedural system*" is not sufficient to invoke this refusal ground.[35] There are six discretionary refusal grounds: (1) the defendant was not duly notified of the proceedings; (2) the judgment was obtained by fraud; (3) the cause of action is against public policy; (4) the judgment conflicts with another conclusive judgment; (5) the judgment was contrary to a forum clause

---

[31] Section 3, second sentence holds that "*The foreign judgment is enforceable in the same manner as the judgment of a sister state which is entitled to full faith and credit*". This has led to some confusion as to whether a foreign judgment is then entitled to the simplified registration procedure that is available for sister state judgments, see Brand 2013, pp. 499–500.

[32] Prefatory note to the 1962 Uniform Foreign Money-Judgments Recognition Act, para 1.

[33] Brand 2013, p. 496.

[34] 1962 Uniform Foreign Money-Judgments Recognition Act, Section 4(a).

[35] The due process analysis was developed by the US Supreme Court in *International Shoe Co. v Washington* 326 US 310, 66 S. Ct. 154 (1945).

agreement between the parties; and (6) the foreign court was a seriously inconvenient forum.[36]

This 1962 Act generally restates principles that have long been established in case law and applied by courts, now allowing states to create a binding, codified legal framework based upon these established principles.[37] A thorough analysis of the application of this Act throughout the US is beyond the scope of this chapter.[38] Just to provide one example, I can refer to the State of New York, which still adheres to provisions based on the 1962 Act.[39] Whereas most provisions in the New York statute are identical to the 1962 Act, there are some differences. The New York statute does list the types of actions that are available to the party requesting recognition, whereas the original text does not.[40] Also, it divides the refusal grounds a little differently, placing 'no jurisdiction over the subject matter' into the category of discretionary grounds rather than obligatory grounds for refusal.[41] Other states have also adopted a form of the 1962 Act in more or less the same manner.

As quite a few states adopted some version of the 1962 Act, it did have a harmonising effect and it specifically includes a section that contains that goal: "*This Act shall be so construed as to effectuate its general purpose to make uniform the law of those states which enact it*".[42] However, states are free to decide to what extent they adopt the provisions or amend them, coming to such uniform law still remains elusive.[43]

3.3.3 The 2005 Uniform Foreign-Country Money Judgments Recognition Act

The 2005 Act (the UFCMJRA) is a revision of the 1962 Act, which contains some significant changes to help meet the demands of ever increasing business relationships worldwide. Most importantly, it clarified certain matters that have led to confusion under the 1962 Act.[44] First, it clarified the burden of proof: the party seeking recognition must show that the judgment falls within the scope of the Act

[36] 1962 Uniform Foreign Money-Judgments Recognition Act, Section 4(b).

[37] Prefatory note to the 1962 Uniform Foreign Money-Judgments Recognition Act, para 2.

[38] For other examples described in more detail, including case law, see Rosner 2004.

[39] New York Civil Practice Law and Rules, § 3501–3509.

[40] In § 5305, being an action on the judgment, a motion for summary judgment, or in a pending action by counterclaim, cross-claim of affirmative defence.

[41] In § 5304.

[42] Section 8.

[43] Rosner 2004, p. 363.

[44] Prefatory note to the 2005 Uniform Foreign-Country Money Judgments Recognition Act, para 2.

and the party opposing recognition must show that one of the refusal grounds is applicable.[45] Furthermore, it contains a statute of limitation, holding that a judgment is not eligible for recognition if it is no longer enforceable in the state of origin, or when a period of 15 years has passed.[46] Thirdly, it addresses procedural issues: when brought as an initial claim, the creditor must file an action for recognition, but recognition can also be raised as a defence to seek preclusive effect or in a counterclaim.[47]

At this moment, 21 states have adopted statutes which correspond with or are at least similar to the 2005 Act. 15 states which beforehand adopted legislation along the lines of the 1962 Act have reviewed their statutes to be more in line with the 2005 Act.[48]

3.3.3.1 Principles for Recognition and Refusal Grounds Under the 2005 UFCMJRA

As far as principles of recognition are concerned, the 2005 Act follows the 1962 Act, with some differences in the discretionary refusal grounds. Section 4(c) under 7 and 8 of the new Act refers to doubtful integrity of the court dealing with the case and insufficiencies in the proceedings as such. This is thus different from the 1962 Act, which does not contain such a provision but only refers to the judicial system as a whole. Furthermore, whilst the 1962 Act solely refers to the cause of action when it comes to the public policy exception, the 2005 Act broadens the scope by not only mentioning the cause of action, but also the judgment itself as contrary to the public policy standards of the state or the US.[49]

Serving as an example, the State of California has adapted its statute to be more in line with the 2005 Act, whereas the originally enacted statute was based on the 1962 Act. It has added an additional discretionary refusal ground for defamation cases. Such a case may be denied recognition if the foreign court did not provide the same amount of protection for free speech as a US court would do.[50] This issue of libel and defamation cases is an issue for the US in general. The problem is the relative ease with which it finds other countries to accept proof in defamation cases which the US is unwilling to recognise. As free speech being protected by the US

---

[45] 2005 Uniform Foreign-Country Money Judgments Recognition Act, Section 3(c) and Section 4(d).

[46] 2005 Uniform Foreign-Country Money Judgments Recognition Act, Section 9.

[47] 2005 Uniform Foreign-Country Money Judgments Recognition Act, Section 6.

[48] Strong 2014, p. 66.

[49] 2005 Uniform Foreign-Country Money Judgments Recognition Act, Section 4(c)(3), see Mondora 2008, p. 1140.

[50] Californian Code of Civil Procedure, § 1716(c): '*The judgment includes recovery for a claim of defamation unless the court determines that the defamation law applied by the foreign court provided at least as much protection for freedom of speech and the press as provided by both the United States and California Constitutions*'.

Constitution is of major importance for the US, a law was passed in 2010 allowing courts to refuse recognition of foreign libel judgments in the US.[51]

As the 2005 Act covers more issues related to recognition and enforcement, there would in principle be a much greater potential harmonising effect. The Act, however, has also led to even more divergence in the law, as not all states which adopted statutes based on the 1962 Act decided to bring those statutes in line with the new Act. Those states who follow the Acts thus have two different instruments from which to choose and can still decide independently to what extent they adhere to the principles.

3.3.4 The Third Restatement

Those states still adhering to common law for the recognition and enforcement mostly rely on parts of the Third Restatement.[52] This Restatement was adopted by the American Law Institute (ALI) in 1986.[53] The most important paragraph is § 481, which holds that "*except as provided in § 482, a final judgment of a court of a foreign state granting or denying recovery of a sum of money, establishing or confirming the status of a person, or determining interests in property, is conclusive between the parties, and is entitled to recognition in courts in the United States*".[54] § 482 lists the mandatory and discretionary refusal grounds, which follow the comity approach as set out in *Hilton*. However, it also rejects the idea of reciprocity. The main difference between the Restatement and the Acts is that the scope of the Restatement is broader, including cases concerning the status of persons or property. Furthermore, the Acts place lack of subject matter jurisdiction under the mandatory refusal grounds, whereas this ground of refusal is discretionary under the Restatement. Also, the 2005 Act contains more discretionary refusal grounds than the Restatement.

Generally, the Restatement compiles common law principles which can be used during an argument and act as persuasive evidence of well-established common law tenets in a US court of law. It is not, however, an instrument that will be adopted as a statute by a state. Therefore, this instrument is more capable of having a sort of bottom-up approach to harmonisation rather than a top-down approach.

---

[51] Securing the Protection of our Enduring and Established Constitutional Heritage (SPEECH) Act, 28 U.S.C, § 4101–4105. New York earlier on changed its statute, see Hay 2009, p. 237. See also Robinson 2013, p. 916.

[52] Restatement (Third) on Foreign Relations Law of the United States, Am. Law Inst. (1987); Brand 2013, p. 500–501. Freedom of speech is discussed below.

[53] The American Law Institute was founded in 1923 to '*promote the clarification and simplification of the law and its better adaptation to social needs, to secure better administration of justice and to encourage and carry out scholarly and scientific work*', see https://www.ali.org/about-ali/creation/. It too is a non-profit organisation made up of professors, lawyers and judges.

[54] Restatement (Third) § 481 and § 482.

3.3.5 *Enforcement of Foreign Money Judgments*

The Acts and principles as described above all concern the recognition phase. As for enforcement, the 1962 Act holds that, when a foreign judgment is recognised, it "*is enforceable in the same manner as the judgment of a sister state which is entitled to full faith and credit*". The 2005 Act holds that the recognised foreign judgment "*is enforceable in the same manner and to the same extent as a judgment rendered in this state*."[55] This means that the actual enforcement as such is not governed by the Acts, but by different procedures at state level. Some confusion has arisen with regard to the relationship between the Acts and the 1964 Revised Uniform Enforcement of Foreign Judgments Act, drafted by the ALI, which covers the enforcement procedure for sister-state judgments.[56] Some courts in states which have adopted both the 1962 and 1964 Act were of the opinion that foreign judgments were also entitled to the simplified registration procedure available under the 1964 Act. However, most courts have held that only the US judgment recognising the foreign judgments is entitled to such treatment, not the foreign judgment itself.[57] The 2005 Act clarifies this point in Section 6 where it is held that "*the issue of recognition shall be raised by filing an action seeking recognition of the foreign country judgment*", making clear that a separate action for recognition is necessary before the enforcement procedure can be commenced.

3.4 Further Attempts to Harmonise the Rules on Recognition and Enforcement

3.4.1 *Preliminary Remarks*

The patchwork of statutes and common law principles as described above does not make it easy for the party seeking recognition and enforcement of a foreign judgment, even if—but mostly because—the differences between states are subtle and sometimes boil down to details.[58] This is what makes recognition and enforcement of judgments particularly challenging. Parties might be less inclined to bring a recognition case in the US as it may not be the most cost-effective, they might fear bias against foreign parties, and in the case of long and complicated court proceedings it might result in certain important transnational issues not being

[55] 2005 Uniform Foreign-Country Money Judgments Recognition Act, Section 3 and Section 7(2).

[56] Uniform Enforcement of Foreign Judgements Act, 13 U.L.A. 149 (1964 revised), (1986), in force in some form or another in almost all states.

[57] Brand 2013, pp. 499–501 and cited case law.

[58] See also Paige 2003, p. 593.

resolved.[59] Despite these issues, in general, scholars agree that the recognition regime of the US is rather liberal compared to that of other countries. Nevertheless, they also all agree that uniformisation or harmonisation of the current regime would benefit the US both at home and during negotiations for possible multilateral frameworks in the future.[60]

3.4.2 The American Law Institute's Proposed Federal Statute

The American Law Institute has also realised that probably the best way to come to a uniform approach, is to enact a federal statute. In 2005, it proposed a federal statute on the recognition and enforcement of foreign money judgments. Such a statute would pre-empt state regulations and contain US-wide standards of procedure and substance.[61] This paragraph will review some of the main differences between the existing regulations at state level and the proposal, which up to this date has not been enacted as federal law in the US.

The proposal contains 13 sections which cover most material issues also covered at the state level. It applies to foreign money judgments, and excludes domestic matters, bankruptcy and (still ongoing) arbitration. It does apply to judgments rendered in succession matters, and taxes, fines and penalties can be recognised on a discretionary basis.[62] The statute also allows for the recognition of default judgments under certain circumstances relating to jurisdiction and proper service, something the Acts and Restatement do not cover.[63] The time limit for an action is 10 years.[64] The proposal provides that the effect of recognition goes beyond the mere liability issue and also covers the fees of the lawyers, other costs and interests.[65]

---

[59] Strong 2014, pp. 87–89.

[60] For example, courts in the EU are less likely to recognise US judgments containing punitive damages awards, see Hay 2009, p. 234. See further Brand 2013, p. 496; Paige 2003, p. 626; Singal 2008, p. 961; Shill 2013, p. 462; Zeynalova 2013, p. 163.

[61] There is a debate on whether it actually comes within the federal competence to regulate this issue, see Strong 2014, p. 93 and the scholarship on the constitutional debate referred to in footnote 193 and 195.

[62] Section 1, at 29 and Section 2 at 35.

[63] Section 3 at 45.

[64] Section 2(c) at 35.

[65] Section 3(a) at 43. Sections 3 and 4 together provide clarity on the (preclusive) effects of recognition, which brings along a form of predictability that does not exist under the Acts or Restatement.

3.4.2.1 Principles for Recognition and Refusal Grounds

In principle, the statute favours recognition and once the conditions are met and the refusal grounds are not applicable, the judgment is to be enforced in accordance with the provisions of the statute, regardless of whether the case was brought in a federal or state court.[66] Section 5 sets out the grounds for refusal which are divided in different groups: mandatory grounds, conflict with a choice of forum and discretionary grounds.

The mandatory grounds are mostly similar to those in the Acts, there are however a couple of important differences. The—discretionary—due process requirement in the 2005 Act relating to the specific case are not reflected in the proposed statute, neither as a mandatory nor as a discretionary ground. The proposed statute's focus lies with the fairness of the judicial system as a whole, which has led to some commentators holding it is less obvious to impose specific US due process values to the case at hand.[67] To balance this, corruption and a lack of integrity of the court are listed as separate mandatory refusal grounds.[68]

Furthermore, recognition is refused if the foreign court assumed jurisdiction based on one of the grounds listed in Section 6.[69] Those grounds all concern instances where the foreign court based jurisdiction on the plaintiff's circumstances—thereby covering a wide range of acceptable jurisdiction grounds outside of the US—deemed unacceptable in the US.[70] The last ground in Section 6 refers to the foreign court having accepted jurisdiction on a ground that is deemed unreasonable or unfair. This is a rather general notion and the ALI explains that the mere fact that the foreign court accepted jurisdiction based on a ground unknown in the US does not as such lead to refusal. However, US principles of unreasonableness or unfairness can be of guidance when the court has to determine whether this refusal ground is appropriate.[71] Another particular feature about this provision is that it can be invoked even if the parties did not challenge jurisdiction in the court of origin.[72] In France for example, it is possible for a court to accept jurisdiction based on the nationality of the plaintiff. The defendant cannot raise that objection in the foreign court. However, it is an unacceptable ground under Section 6 and recognition can thus be challenged in a US court.

Furthermore, there are mandatory grounds that concern proper notice, fraud, and public policy. These grounds, for the most part, reflect those in the Acts, with the

---

[66] Section 2(a) at 35.

[67] Section 5(c) at 58; Carodine 2007, p. 1234; Rosen 2004, pp. 186–209.

[68] Section 5(d) at 60.

[69] Section 5(a)(iii) at 55, which refers to Section 6, at 84.

[70] These are jurisdiction based on: mere presence of property of the defendant; the plaintiff's nationality, domicile, residence or place of incorporation; the mere fact that the defendant was in transit in a certain state when he was served; any other basis deemed unfair. See Silberman 2006, pp. 1433–1434.

[71] Strong 2014, pp. 125–126.

[72] Section 6(d), at 87.

difference of being discretionary there rather than mandatory in the proposal. Simply put, the ALI proposal contains more mandatory refusal grounds than the Acts or Restatement.

Concerning the discretionary grounds, these include lack of subject matter jurisdiction, irreconcilability with another foreign judgment, proceedings that were initiated in the foreign court after the same action between the same parties was initiated in the US, and foreign proceedings that were only initiated to frustrate the other party's possibilities to bring the claim in a US court.[73] Note here that subject matter jurisdiction is a mandatory ground under the Acts. Also, irreconcilability is only mentioned with regard to other foreign judgments in this proposal. If the foreign judgment is conflicting with another US judgment, the US judgment will prevail under the Full Faith and Credit Clause.[74]

3.4.2.2 The Pros and Cons of the Proposed Statute

Needless to say, the harmonising effects of this statute would be significant, leading to more consistency and uniformity in the scattered landscape. A federal statute pre-empting state law is the most obvious way to come to harmonisation. It would then follow the example of the European Union, where such an instrument has—successfully—existed for many years in the form of the Brussels-regime.

There are some clear improvements in this statute, mostly in the form of clarifications, as compared to the Acts or Restatement. First of all, it applies to declaratory judgments and injunctions—be it on a discretionary basis, types of judgments that are excluded in the Acts and Restatement. Second, the effects of recognition and the recognition of default judgments is clarified. Third, the proposal clarifies the burden of proof, which only the 2005 Act has a provision on. It is also clearer on the procedure to be followed.

One particular feature, however, has not been received so positively: the reciprocity requirement.[75] Expressly excluded from the Acts or Restatement, it is present in the ALI proposal. The burden of proof lies with the party opposing recognition, showing that "*there is substantial doubt that the courts of the state of origin would grant recognition or enforcement to comparable judgments of courts in the United States*."[76] The provision then lists certain factors which the court takes into account when looking at reciprocity and it entails some exceptions.[77] According to the comment accompanying Section 7(b), this requirement was added

[73] Section 5(c) at 57.

[74] US Constitution Article IV, para 1.

[75] Strong 2014, p. 127 and the scholarship referred to in footnote 395; Zeynalova 2013, p. 203. Also contra see McFarland 2011, pp. 96–100. However, see pro-reciprocity Ballard 2006, pp. 199–238.

[76] Section 7(b).

[77] Strong 2014, p. 129.

to give an incentive to foreign states to recognise US judgments. It is true that some major trading partners of the US still have a reciprocity requirement in their national law, which could lead to US judgments being treated less favourably than judgments coming from those countries in the US.[78] It has however been suggested that leaving out such a requirement would be "leading by example", which in itself would be sufficient incentive for other countries to recognise US judgments.[79] Including a reciprocity requirement might lead to a situation in which claims that deserve to be recognised based on fairness, are not being recognised when the reciprocity argument is successfully made; a matter which is, in for example tort cases, left to the discretion of the judge.[80] In general, without empirical evidence, it is going to be difficult for a court to establish whether a foreign court will or will not recognise comparable US judgments. This clause thus leads to unpredictability, which is unfortunate.[81]

3.4.3 Is Harmonisation the Way Forward for the US' Recognition and Enforcement Regime?

The answer to the question whether the US should move forward and adopt a federal statute should in my opinion be answered in the affirmative. Where, in the past, general corporate litigation strategies included creating long delays in recognition procedures and a complex patchwork of different regulations, that idea has slowly been replaced by the realisation that a more uniform approach is in the corporation's best interest in the long run.[82] Also, even though indisputable empirical evidence does not exist at this time, the reported problems relating to delays, possible bias, costs and unpredictability do exist.[83] However, before harmonisation by way of federal statute would make sense, a couple of outstanding issues have to be resolved, including reciprocity as discussed above.[84]

A factor that leads to unpredictability for the parties in the Acts, Restatement and the statute proposed by the ALI, is the "due process" requirement. An examination of the foreign procedure in that regard might lead to an increase in the amount of relitigation of cases, an outcome which would interfere with the overall goal of a recognition regime meant to avoid this. In general, a due process requirement

[78] Singal 2008, pp. 954–955.

[79] Singal 2008, p. 971.

[80] Singal 2008, pp. 962–963; Strong 2014, p. 129.

[81] See the suggestions made by Singal in his paper for a bright-line reciprocity agreement, p. 975, and in the end suggesting that this requirement is dropped, pp. 977–978.

[82] See Weston 2011, p. 736; Strong 2014, p. 143; Zeynalova 2013, p. 169 and the references in footnote 121.

[83] Zeynalova 2013, p. 152 and further.

[84] Contra adoption of the ALI proposed statute see McFarland 2011, pp. 63–100.

imposes a burden upon the parties and court: how exactly and to what extent does a US court evaluate the functioning of a foreign legal system and court procedure? Which factors determine whether a system is considered good or bad?[85] Different courts approach the due process requirement differently, making it difficult to predict the outcome of such an argument in court.[86] In my opinion the proposed statute could have provided a clearer line to follow in determining the due process requirement.

Another feature of the current system is that once a judgment is recognised by a US court—which has to be done in a separate proceeding—that judgment has to be enforced in all other States under the Full Faith and Credit Clause.[87] This process is referred to as "domestication."[88] This can lead to forum shopping, namely finding a jurisdiction that is most likely to recognise the foreign judgment after which it is transformed into a US judgments and enjoys the accompanying benefits. For a court to hear a recognition case, it is not necessary that the assets concerned are located in that state, making forum shopping possible.[89] For example, as Florida has a reciprocity requirement in its statutes, a party could be more inclined to seek recognition elsewhere and enforcement in Florida afterwards. Adopting a federal statute would reduce this kind of forum shopping.

Especially because of this feature, one scholar has proposed a very different approach to the uniformisation of the recognition and enforcement regime. He suggests that the US should not strive for harmonisation via codification, but instead strive for uniformisation via a voluntary method of coordination.[90] This would entail that courts are allowed to apply their own law to the recognition judgment at the enforcement stage and could lead to a court refusing to enforce the underlying judgment if it would not have recognised it in the first place.[91] Where he is of the opinion that in the short term this might lead to more discrepancies, in the long run it should lead to a more uniform national recognition and enforcement regime. This approach seems to be far-fetched as it relies on a voluntary method, making the insecurity of the realisation of the wanted result significant.

3.4.3.1 A Global Level of Harmonisation—The Hague Conventions

Next to harmonisation at national level, there is a development at the global level in the form of the Hague Convention on Choice of Court Agreements, which the US

[85] Stephan 2014, p. 84.

[86] Weston 2011, pp. 741–747.

[87] *Nadd v Le Credit Lyonnais* S.A., 804 So.2d 1226, 1231–33 (2001).

[88] Little 2013, p. 952.

[89] Brand 2013, p. 506 and discussed case law.

[90] Shill 2013, p. 471.

[91] Shill 2013, p. 464.

signed in 2009, but has not yet ratified.[92] It is the first multilateral treaty containing provisions on recognition and enforcement to which the US is a party. Article 9 contains the refusal grounds which largely correspond to those in the Acts and Restatement, with the exception of the jurisdictional grounds. Instead, recognition has to be refused in case the forum clause was invalid. This Convention provides for an easier and more secure way of recognition and enforcement of judgments in case of an exclusive choice of forum agreement. It means that when foreign parties enter into such an agreement, they can rely on the rules laid down in this Convention when they find themselves in a US court for recognition or enforcement —had the US ratified. For business purposes this Convention is thus an improvement, leading to more security and predictability for the parties. It would be a nice step forward for the US if they were to ratify this Convention. The ULC has been asked to draft legislation in this regard and came up with a final text in 2012, however, with a fierce debate on which form this piece of legislation should take—federal-only or not—this text has not been adopted by Congress.[93]

Furthermore, there is the ongoing Judgments Project, an ambitious undertaking for the Hague Conference to come to a Convention on recognition and enforcement of foreign judgments.[94] It has been ongoing for more than 20 years and it will take many more before a Convention is signed, let alone ratified. Especially during the negotiations for this Convention, the differences in approaching jurisdictional matters between the civil law countries and the common law countries have become evident and are the main reason why the Convention has not yet seen a final text.[95] More coherence in the recognition regime at national level can lead to a stronger position of the US during the remainder of the negotiations, another reason why adoption of a federal statute could be beneficial for the US. The ALI realised this, as initial failure of the Hague Judgments Projects worked as an incentive to create the proposed statute.[96]

3.5 Conclusion

The current recognition and enforcement regime in the US can be summarised as consisting of 50 different regimes. Despite the efforts of the Uniform Law Commission and the American Law Institute, we cannot conclude that the US has

[92] To be found in the status table on https://www.hcch.net/en/instruments/conventions/specialised-sections/choice-of-court.

[93] See all drafts and further information on http://www.uniformlaws.org/Committee.aspx?title=Choice%20of%20Court%20Agreements%20Convention%20Implementation%20Act.

[94] For all information regarding this project, see https://www.hcch.net/en/projects/legislative-projects/judgments.

[95] Silberman 2000, p. 639; Burbank 2001, pp. 204–206 and further discussion on lis pendens, forum non conveniens and anti-suit injunctions; Murphy 2001, pp. 418–421.

[96] Silberman and Lowenfeld 2000, p. 635.

harmonised rules for the recognition and enforcement of foreign money judgments in the traditional sense, as there is no federal statute. As most scholar agree, such harmonisation is called for. The federal government adopting the ALI proposed statute would provide the path of least resistance for the US. Even though it is in principle pro-recognition, there are sufficient provisions that can limit that general approach. As stated above, harmonisation will lead to more predictability and more stability which will be beneficial for parties finding themselves in a situation of international litigation.

As the US Congress continues to delay ratification of the Hague Choice of Court Convention and the fact that the Hague Judgments Project will take many more years, focusing on recognition and enforcement at the national level is the most sensible thing to do. As is the case for any national, bilateral or multilateral agreement however, they can only come into existence with political will. With the new administration off to a turbulent start, the priorities of the government at this moment—however understandably—unfortunately lie elsewhere.

References

Ballard FO (2006) Turnabout Is Fair Play: Why a Reciprocity Requirement Should Be Included in the American Law Institute's Proposed Federal Statute. Hous. J. Int. L., 28:199–238

Brand R (2013) Recognition and Enforcement of Foreign Judgments. U. Pitt. L. Rev., 74:491–549

Burbank S (2001) Jurisdictional Equilibration, the Proposed Hague Convention and Progress in National Law. Am. J. Comp. L., 49:203–248

Burnham W (2011) Introduction to the law and legal system of the United States. West Academic, St. Paul, Minnesota

Carodine MD (2007) Political Judging: When Due Process Goes International. Wm. & Mary L. Rev., 48:1159–1246

Dickinson A (2015) Background and Introduction to the Regulation. In: Dickinson A et al (eds) The Brussels I Regulation Recast. Oxford University Press, New York, pp 1–54

Hay P (2009) Conflict of Laws, Cases and Materials. Thompson Reuters, New York

Little L (2013) Conflict of Laws: Cases Materials and Problems. Wolters Kluwer, New York

Magnus U (2016) Introduction. In: Magnus U et al (eds) European Commentaries on Private International Law – Brussels Ibis Regulation. Otto Schmidt, Köln, pp 1–53

McFarland RL (2011) Federalism, Finality, and Foreign Judgments: Examining the ALI Judgments Project's Proposed Federal Foreign Judgments Statute. New Eng. L. Rev., 45:63–100

Mondora C (2008) The Public Policy Exception, "The Freedom of Speech, or of the Press", and the Uniform Foreign-Country Money Judgments Recognition Act. Hofstra L. Rev., 36:1139–1175

Murphy D (2001) Negotiation of Convention on Jurisdiction and Enforcement of Judgments. Am. J. Int'L., 95:387–421

Paige BR (2003) Foreign Judgments in American and English Courts: A Comparative Analysis. Seattle U. L. Rev., 26:591–626

Robinson DJ (2013) U.S. Enforcement of Foreign Judgments, Libel Tourism, and the SPEECH Act: Protecting Speech or Discouraging Foreign Legal Cooperation? Transnat'l L. & Contemp. Probs., 21:911–933

Rosen MD (2004) Exporting the Constitution. Emory L.J., 53:186-209

Rosner N (2004) Cross-Border Recognition and Enforcement of Foreign Money Judgments in Civil and Commercial Matters. Dissertation. Ulrik Hubert Institute for Private International Law, Groningen

Sachs S (2009) Full Faith and Credit in the Early Congress. Va. L. Rev., 95:1201–1279

Schmitt J (2013) Historical Reassessment of Full Faith and Credit. Geo Mason L. Rev., 20:485–544

Shill G (2013) Ending Judgment Arbitrage: Jurisdictional Competition and the Enforcement of Foreign Money Judgments in the United States. Harv. Int'l L.J. 54:459–522

Silberman LJ (2006) Transnational Litigation: Is There A "Field"? A Tribute to Hal Maier. V and. J. Transnat'l L., 39:1427–1437

Silberman LJ, Lowenfeld AF (2000) A Different Challenge for the ALI: Herein of Foreign Country Judgments, an International Treaty, and an American Statute. Indiana L. J. 75:635–647

Singal V (2008) Preserving Power Without Sacrificing Justice: Creating an Effective Reciprocity Regime for the Recognition and Enforcement of Foreign Judgments. Hastings L.J. 59:943–977

Stephan PB (2014) Foreign Court Judgments and the United States Legal System. Brill Nijhoff, Leiden/Boston

Story J (1834) Commentaries on the Conflict of Laws. Hilliard, Gray, and Company, Boston

Strong SI (2014) Recognition and Enforcement of Foreign Judgments in US Courts: Problems and Possibilities. Rev. Litig., 33:45–146

Weston C (2011) The Enforcement Loophole: Judgment-Recognition Defenses as a Loophole to Corporate Accountability for Conduct Abroad. Emory Int'l L. Rev., 25:731–770

Zeynalova Y (2013) The Law on Recognition and Enforcement of Foreign Judgments: Is It Broken and How Do We Fix It? Berkeley J. Int'L., 31:150–206

Chapter 4
The Harmonisation of Interim Measures Granted by the Emergency Arbitrator in the European Union

Junmin Zhang

Contents

Abstract Interim measures play an important role in protecting parties' rights in international commercial arbitration. The emergency arbitrator mechanism provides a possibility to seek interim measures before the constitution of the arbitral tribunal

---

Junmin Zhang, Ph.D candidate at Maastricht University, Faculty of Law, P.O. Box 616, 6200 MD Maastricht, the Netherlands, junmin.zhang@maastrichtuniversity.nl, 0031433882222.
The research is sponsored by the China Scholarship Council.

J. Zhang (✉)
Faculty of Law, Maastricht University, P.O. Box 616, 6200 MD, Maastricht, The Netherlands
e-mail: junmin.zhang@maastrichtuniversity.nl

V. Lazić and S. Stuij (eds.), *International Dispute Resolution*,
Short Studies in Private International Law,
https://doi.org/10.1007/978-94-6265-252-1_4

without going to state courts. The mechanism has been recognized and adopted by various arbitral institutions. However, owing to the lack of unified regulation in this field, the uncertainty and unpredictability remain regarding the mechanism. This article aims to address the necessity and possibility of harmonisation of the interim measures granted by the emergency arbitrator in the European Union (EU). First, it gives a general introduction regarding the interim measures and the emergency arbitrator mechanism. The basic framework of the emergency arbitrator mechanism and the current legislation within the EU regarding interim measures are discussed in the following part. It then explores the necessity and possibility of harmonisation in the emergency arbitrator mechanisms in the EU. Finally, a proposal for such harmonisation is suggested for a more effective international commercial arbitration system in the EU.

Keywords Interim measures · Emergency Arbitrator · International commercial arbitration · Enforcement · Harmonisation · European Union

4.1 Introduction

In guaranteeing the commercial rights of the parties and the enforcement of final awards, interim measures are essentially important in modern arbitration. Usually, when the extreme urgency happens before the constitution of the tribunal, parties have to go to state courts to apply for interim measures, which may violate the primary willingness to solve the dispute in arbitration. The legal institute of what is called "emergency arbitrator" is a mechanism trying to save this dilemma by providing a sole emergency arbitrator from the arbitral institution for issuing the interim measures. However, so far there is no harmonized regulation governing the interim measures granted by the emergency arbitrator.

"[A] unique economic and political union between 28 European countries"[1] covers most of the continent of Europe. The EU has achieved many outstanding results in uniformity and harmonisation. One important part is in the law. This article would discuss specifically the necessity and possibility of the harmonisation of interim measures granted by the emergency arbitrator in international commercial arbitration in the dimension of the EU in order to meet the objectives of the Union, and to promote the EU as a more arbitration-friendly region.

4.1.1 The Use of Interim Measures

Interim measures, also known as "provisional measures", "conservatory measures", "emergency relief", "interim relief", or "preliminary injunctions", are used to ensure

[1] European Union 2017, para 1.

that the "substantive rights are not frustrated during the wait for the final decision",[2] and they "have an undeniable contractual value".[3] When it comes to international transactions which may become extremely complicated, the need for interim measures is increasing. Interim measures can achieve "final and significant consequences",[4] avoiding a meaningless arbitral award.[5]

Generally, the forms of interim measures in practice are broad.[6] The bottom line lies on the arbitral agreement and the mandatory regulations in national arbitration law. For example, the frequently employed interim measures in international commercial arbitration include the ones protecting or maintaining the *status quo* until the final decision, facilitating the arbitral proceedings, preserving the assets in order to satisfy the final enforcement of an award, and reserving the relevant evidence for the unsettled dispute.[7]

4.1.2 The Bodies to Grant Interim Measures

Usually, when the parties need the interim measures during the process of arbitration, they would go to state courts, or wait until the constitution of the arbitral tribunal.

In the 2015 International Arbitration Survey: Improvements and Innovations in International Arbitration conducted jointly by Queen Mary University of London and White & Case LLP, it was indicated that 46% of respondents would prefer to seek interim measures from state courts.[8] It is quite obvious that going to courts has its irreplaceable benefit, meaning that the courts have coercive power not only to grant, but also to enforce interim measures. Additionally, courts can order interim measures against third parties. However, under certain circumstances, courts would not be favoured for the following reasons. Firstly, when the dispute goes to a domestic court, then the case would be public. Confidentiality would not be guaranteed. Secondly, going to court for interim measures may violate the preference that parties can solve the dispute in a peaceful way in the first place. Thirdly, it is very hard to choose the neutral court, especially in international disputes which value the impartiality in resolution. Sometimes, conflicting judgments may occur because of multiple jurisdictions in several states[9] as well.

---

[2] European Parliament's Committee on Legal Affairs 2014, p. 49.

[3] Mohmeded 2016, p. 45.

[4] UNCITRAL Working Group on Arbitration 2000a, para 66.

[5] UNCITRAL Working Group on Arbitration 2000b, para 7; Bucy 2010, p. 584.

[6] Born 2014, p. 2483.

[7] UNCITRAL Model Law on International Commercial Arbitration 2006, Article 17(2); Athhan 2011, p. 207; Yesilirmak 2005, pp. 10–12; Moses 2012, p. 101.

[8] Queen Mary University of London and White & Case LLP 2015, p. 27.

[9] Savola 2015, p. 2.

Historically speaking, “national law has not infrequently denied arbitrators the power to order interim measures”[10] based on the rationale that arbitrators could not issue coercive measures with the concern of public policy.[11] However, with the development of international arbitration and the increasing need for interim measures, “[s]tates began to view the courts’ role as supportive of arbitration, rather than considering them separately”.[12] The prohibition for arbitrators to grant interim measures has “rightly been almost universally abandoned”.[13]

Although the arbitral tribunal lacks the power to enforce interim measures judicially, voluntary compliance is usually seen. According to the 2012 International Arbitration Survey: Current and Preferred Practices in the Arbitral Process by Queen Mary University of London and White & Case LLP, 62% of the interim measures were complied with by the parties themselves[14] and “on average, parties seek enforcement by a court in only 10% of interim measures applications which are granted by the arbitral tribunal”.[15] The reason for the high level of compliance is simple, because parties would not tend to “put themselves in a disadvantageous position through wrongful conducts”[16] before winning the battle.

Nevertheless, waiting for the constitution of the arbitral tribunal will be time-consuming and could cause serious consequences, such as eliminated evidence, or irreparable harm which may lead to meaningless final awards. To prevent these, some arbitral institutions developed various mechanisms in order to grant fast and valid interim measures without the necessity to go to state courts.

In 1990, the International Court of Arbitration of the International Chamber of Commerce (ICC) introduced a set of rules to give parties the possibility of interim measures before the constitution of the tribunal, namely the Rules for a Pre-Arbitral Referee Procedure. Unfortunately, mainly due to the opt-in approach adopted,[17] the procedure is barely used, and even unknown to most of the public.[18]

In 1999, the American Arbitration Association (AAA) created the Optional Rules for Emergency Measures of Protection. Similar to the ICC Rules for a Pre-Arbitral Referee Procedure, the AAA Optional Rules used the same opt-in approach, which led to difficulties in practice by requiring the parties to agree on these rules separately.[19]

In 2006, the International Centre for Dispute Resolution (ICDR)—which is an international branch of AAA—developed the emergency arbitrator in its

---

[10] Born 2014, p. 2432.

[11] Bucy 2010, p. 588.

[12] Ibid.

[13] Born 2014, p. 2432.

[14] Queen Mary University of London and White & Case LLP 2012, p. 2.

[15] Ibid., p. 17.

[16] Athhan 2011, p. 210.

[17] ICC Rules for a Pre-Arbitral Referee Procedure 1990, Article 2.1.1.

[18] Born 2014, p. 2451; Gaillard and Pinsolle 2004, p. 13.

[19] Lemenez and Quigley 2008, p. 2; Smith 2016, p. 2.

International Dispute Resolution Procedures 2006. The Procedures were amended in 2014, in which ICDR followed the opt-out solution for the emergency arbitrator provisions. After nearly ten years' development, most of the world's leading international arbitral institutions like the Arbitration Institute of the Stockholm Chamber of Commerce (SCC), the ICC, the London Court of International Arbitration (LCIA), the Singapore International Arbitration Centre (SIAC) and the Hong Kong International Arbitration Centre (HKIAC) have adopted the emergency arbitrator mechanism.

4.1.3 The Desirability of the Emergency Arbitrator Mechanism

The emergency arbitrator mechanism is used when applied for by the parties, to grant interim measures before the constitution of the arbitral tribunal, without prejudging the merits of the dispute in a short time period. 93% of respondents in the 2015 International Arbitration Survey: Improvements and Innovations in International Arbitration favoured the emergency arbitration to be included in arbitration institutional rules.[20] 38% of them even preferred it to act as a mandatory role.[21] Behind this preference and wide acceptance, the emergency arbitrator mechanism has its unique advantages.

Firstly, the emergency arbitrator mechanism is highly efficient, which is the priority in issuing the interim measures when meeting urgency. According to SCC Arbitration Rules 2017, the appointment of an emergency arbitrator shall be made within 24 h and the decision of the emergency arbitrator shall be made within 5 days after the referred application.[22] Additionally, the challenge of an emergency arbitrator shall be made within 24 h.[23] In action, the statistics show that in all relevant SCC cases in 2016, the emergency arbitrator was appointed within 24 hours, and the median days for an emergency arbitrator decision since referral is 6 days.[24]

In comparison to the constitution of the tribunal, the process in SCC Arbitration Rules 2017 is within 10 days for a sole arbitrator and a stipulated time for more than one arbitrator.[25] The challenge shall be raised within 15 days when the circumstance is known to the parties.[26] The tribunal is supposed to grant the final award

---

[20] Queen Mary University of London and White & Case LLP 2015, p. 29.

[21] Ibid.

[22] Appendix II, SCC Arbitration Rules 2017, Appendix II, Article 4 and 8.

[23] SCC Arbitration Rules 2017, Appendix II, Article 4.

[24] SCC 2017, Emergency Arbitrator Proceedings 2016.

[25] SCC Arbitration Rules 2017, Article 17.

[26] SCC Arbitration Rules 2017, Article 19.

within 6 months.[27] However, usually, the time limit is extended, as it is shown in SCC statistics, the majority of cases administrated under the SCC commenced in 2016 "took between 6 and 12 months from the time of registration of a case until the rendering of an award".[28]

Secondly, the emergency arbitrator mechanism guarantees the confidentiality and impartiality of the process. The emergency arbitrator is appointed by the arbitral institution, which is neutral. The parties are also given the right to challenge an improper appointment.[29] Meanwhile, the application of the emergency arbitrator in issuing the interim measures instead of going to state courts respects the initial willingness of parties to resolve the disputes without the case going to public.

Thirdly, the emergency arbitrator is easily accessible. Unlike the ICC Rules for a Pre-arbitral Referee Procedure, the emergency arbitrator provisions are contained in the institutional rules, which means the mechanism is a part of the arbitral rules. If the parties do not exclude the emergency arbitrator provisions, the mechanism will automatically apply.[30] Additionally, the application of emergency arbitrator does not require the knowledge of another unfamiliar legal system and procedure. Spending extra time and effort on a foreign legislation may end up with the delay of interim measures leading to a meaningless final award.

With all the advantages discussed above, the desirability of the emergency arbitrator mechanism for interim measures in international commercial arbitration is understandable. Like every other mechanism has practical problems, the emergency arbitrator is no exception. In the following chapter, the current situation of interim measures concerning an emergency arbitrator mechanism within the EU will be evaluated in detail.

4.2 Overview of the Current Situation in Interim Measures Granted by the Emergency Arbitrator in the EU

The rules regulating the interim measures by the emergency arbitrator exist for most leading arbitral institutions. The analysis will focus on the institutions based in the EU. For national arbitration law of Member States, since there is fewer concerning emergency arbitrators, the discussion will put mainly on the interim measures in general.

---

[27] SCC Arbitration Rules 2017, Article 43.

[28] SCC 2017, Time for Rendering Award.

[29] ICC Arbitration Rules 2017, Appendix V, Article 3; SCC Arbitration Rules 2017, Appendix II, Article 4.

[30] Boog 2013, p. 815.

4.2.1 Leading EU Arbitral Institutions' Emergency Arbitrator Provisions

"[T]he five most preferred arbitral institutions are the ICC, the LCIA, the HKIAC, the SIAC and the SCC".[31] The emergency arbitrator provisions in the arbitral rules of the ICC, the LCIA and the SCC, which are based in EU Member States, will be discussed as examples.

The ICC brought the emergency arbitrator mechanism into its arbitration rules on 1 January 2012. Article 29 and Appendix V of the ICC Arbitration Rules 2012 regulate the emergency arbitrator procedures. The new ICC Arbitration Rules 2017 came into force from 1 March 2017. There is nothing substantial changed concerning the emergency arbitrator provisions. LCIA introduced the mechanism with the amendments in Article 9B in 1 October 2014. The SCC started to use the provisions concerning emergency arbitrator in 1 January 2010. New SCC Arbitration Rules 2017 still used the same approach, only with the increasing fees.

4.2.1.1 Recent Statistics in Practicing Emergency Arbitrator Mechanism

The ICC is a world famous international arbitration centre based in Paris, France, which is "recognized and respected as the benchmark for international dispute resolution".[32] There are 78 applications for the emergency arbitrator proceedings applied since the amendment in total.[33]

The LCIA received two applications for the emergency arbitrator proceedings since the 2014 amendment of its new arbitration rules.[34]

The SCC administrated three emergency arbitrator cases in 2017,[35] and 13 emergency arbitrator proceedings in 2016.[36] Of the 13 cases, seven requests have been granted interim measures, the other six were denied. Nine of the decisions were in the form of an order, and four were emergency arbitrator awards. Comparing to the statistics in 2014–2015, during which years there were only five emergency arbitrator proceedings, the claim for interim measures from the emergency arbitrator is increasing.[37]

---

[31] Queen Mary University of London and White & Case LLP 2015, p. 2.

[32] ICC 2017, para 1.

[33] ICC 2018, Emergency Arbitrator.

[34] LCIA 2014, p. 5; LCIA 2015, p. 5; LCIA 2016, p. 14; LCIA 2017, p. 18.

[35] SCC 2018, Emergency Arbitrator Proceedings 2017.

[36] SCC 2017, Emergency Arbitrator Proceedings 2016.

[37] SCC 2016, p. 7.

4.2.1.2 Emergency Arbitrator Proceedings

In general, the emergency arbitrator procedures in different arbitral institutions are similar based on the "common, general procedural framework".[38]

In order to start an emergency arbitrator proceeding, an application is necessary to the arbitral institution. The information and documentation needed varies from institution to institution. The shared element is that the party needs to state the specific urgent claim in request. After the application, the arbitral institution will assess the jurisdiction of the emergency arbitrator based on a *prima facie* standard.[39] If the application is granted, then the proceedings moves to the next ground —appointment of the emergency arbitrator. In the ICC Arbitration Rules 2017, the appointment needs to be made within 2 days since the receipt of the application.[40] The LCIA Arbitration Rules 2014 provide for 3 days' appointment[41] and the SCC Arbitration Rules 2017 require the appointment to be made within 24 h.[42] A challenge for the emergency arbitrator is possible due to the lack of impartiality, lack of independence and other reasons.[43]

There is no specific standard for the emergency arbitrator to grant interim measures. The ICC Arbitration Rules 2017 state that the emergency arbitrator "shall conduct the proceedings in the manner which the emergency arbitrator considers to be appropriate, taking into the account the nature and the urgency".[44] The LCIA Arbitration Rules 2014 and SCC Arbitration Rules 2017 adopt similar wording.[45] It is believed that without giving specific requirements, the emergency arbitrator may have more discretion for the typical nature of interim measures.

The final decision of the emergency arbitrator can take the form of an order or an award. The ICC specifies that an emergency arbitrator decision under ICC rules shall be an "order".[46] The LCIA accepts both forms.[47] The SCC does not regulate this aspect, using the term "decisions".[48] The SCC Arbitration Rules 2017 set up the 5-day time limit for the emergency arbitrator to decide on the case,[49] ICC goes

[38] Santacroce 2015, p. 285.

[39] ICC Arbitration Rules 2017, Appendix V, Article 1(5); LCIA Arbitration Rules 2014, Article 9.6.

[40] ICC Arbitration Rules 2017, Appendix V, Article 2(1).

[41] LCIA Arbitration Rules 2014, Article 9.6.

[42] SCC Arbitration Rules 2017, Appendix II, Article 4(1).

[43] ICC Arbitration Rules 2017, Appendix V, Article 3(1); LCIA Arbitration Rules 2014, Article 9.6; SCC Arbitration Rules 2017, Appendix II, Article 4(3).

[44] ICC Arbitration Rules 2017, Appendix V, Article 5(2).

[45] LCIA Arbitration Rules 2014, Article 9.7; SCC Arbitration Rules 2017, Appendix II, Article 7.

[46] ICC Arbitration Rules 2017, Appendix V, Article 6(1).

[47] LCIA Arbitration Rules 2014, Article 9.8.

[48] SCC Arbitration Rules 2017, Appendix II, Article 8.

[49] SCC Arbitration Rules 2017, Appendix II, Article 8(1).

with 15 days[50] and the LCIA regulates for 14 days.[51] All the decisions are binding for the parties, but could be revised, or terminated by the later arbitral tribunal.

Besides the common grounds, there are some unique different features. The LCIA is the only institution accepting the *ex parte* emergency relief in Article 9.7 stating that the emergency arbitrator has the power under certain circumstance to decide the interim measures without consulting the respondent.[52] The SCC applies the "opt-out feature in respect of the EA [emergency arbitrator] provisions retroactively",[53] which allows the parties to use the mechanism even before the commencement of the adoption of the emergency arbitrator provision.

4.2.2 EU Member States' Arbitration Laws

Unfortunately, there is no express provision on emergency arbitrators existing in the national legislations in EU Member States. The regulations on interim measures vary from state to state. Even the power of the state courts and arbitral tribunals is different.

In most EU Member States, interim measures are available from both an arbitral tribunal and a state court. In Article 585 and 593 of the Austrian Code of Civil Procedure 2014, the power to issue interim measures is given to both arbitral tribunals and courts. In the Belgian Arbitration Act 2013, Article 1683 and 1691, the tribunals and courts share the power to grant interim measures. Situations are similar in Articles 9 and 21 of the Bulgarian Law on International Commercial Arbitration 2008, Articles 16 and 44 of the Croatian Law on Arbitration 2001, Articles 9 and 17 of the Cyprus International Commercial Arbitration Law 1987, Sections 9 and 17 of the Danish Arbitration Act 2005, Article 731 Estonia Code of Civil Procedure 2013, Articles 1449 and 1468 of the French Code of Civil Procedure 2011, Sections 1033 and 1041 of the German Arbitral Proceedings Reform Act 1998, Sections 26 and 37 of the Hungarian Act LCCI of 1994 on Arbitration, Articles 9 and 17 of the Irish Arbitration Act 2010, Article 1241 of the Luxembourg New Code of Civil Procedure 1998, Articles 61 and 62 of the Malta Arbitration Act 2015, Articles 1166 and 1181 of the Polish Civil Procedure code 1964, Articles 585 and 1117 of the Romanian Civil Procedure Code, Sections 2 and 22 of the Slovak Act on Arbitration 2002 and Section 25 of the Swedish Arbitration Act 1999.

In the Arbitration Act 1996 of the United Kingdom, only when the parties agree, the arbitral tribunal has the jurisdiction and power to provide interim measures.

---

[50] ICC Arbitration Rules 2017, Appendix V, Article 6(4).

[51] LCIA Arbitration Rules 2014, Article 9.8.

[52] LCIA Arbitration Rules 2014, Article 9.7.

[53] Bose and Meredith 2012, p. 190.

In Act 60/2003 of 23 December 2013 on Arbitration of Spain, both arbitral tribunals and courts can grant interim measures and the powers in respect of interim measures are alternative and concurrent.

The Lithuania Law of Commercial Arbitration 1996 shares the power between arbitral tribunals and courts. Meanwhile under Article 25 and 26, the ruling of arbitral tribunals on interim measures, not only domestic ones but also the ones made in other states, may be recognized and enforced. In the Portuguese Voluntary Arbitration Law 2011 and the Law on Arbitration of Slovenia 2008, the enforcement of interim measures is possible as well.

The newly amended Dutch Code of Civil Procedure in 2015 provides parties the possibility to authorize a separate arbitral tribunal to grant provisional relief at the request of the parties.[54] It is considered that Dutch law implies the possibility to apply the emergency arbitrator mechanism for interim measures needed. Additionally, the interim measures shall be considered as enforceable arbitral awards under Dutch law.[55]

Under Section 22 of the Czech Arbitration Act 1994 and Article 818 of the Italian Code of Civil Procedure, state courts have the exclusive power to grant interim measures. The Finland Arbitration Act 2015 does not empower the arbitral tribunal to render interim measures. Article 889 of the Greek Code of Civil Procedure 1995 and Article 17 of the Greek 2735/1999 Law on International Commercial Arbitration say that only in the case of international commercial arbitration, interim measures are possible from arbitral tribunals. In Latvia Civil Procedure Law 2007, state courts can only issue interim measures for security before the constitution of the tribunal. During arbitral proceedings, neither the tribunal, nor state courts can grant such relief.[56]

4.3 Necessity of Harmonisation in Arbitral Interim Measures in the EU

Despite all of the advantages of an emergency arbitrator mechanism, there is always an Achilles' heel, *i.e.* the enforceability. This fatal problem asks for the recognition and enforcement of national arbitration law or the harmonisation and uniformity of arbitration laws concerning interim measures. Taking the goal of integration of the EU, said harmonisation is necessary.

---

[54] Dutch Code of Civil Procedure 2015, Article 1043b(2) and Article 1043b(4).

[55] Van Haersolte-Van Hof 2014, p. 430; Santacroce 2015, p. 309.

[56] Kačevska 2014, Interaction of national courts and tribunals.

4.3.1 The Previous Debate Against Harmonisation in Arbitration

There is no regulation in EU law concerning the international commercial arbitration currently. Arbitration is expressly excluded in Regulation (EU) No 1215/2012 on jurisdiction and the recognition and enforcement of judgments in civil and commercial matters Recast (Brussels I Recast). Article 1(2)(d) of the Brussels I Recast provides that the regulations shall not apply to arbitration.

The rationale behind this exclusion because of the fact that all EU Member States are parties to the Convention on the Recognition and Enforcement of Foreign Arbitral Awards 1958 (New York Convention) and most of them are parties to the European Convention on International Arbitration 1961. There seems to be no need for further regulation. The Explanatory Statement of the Draft Report on 20 June 2011 of the Committee of Legal Affairs of the European Parliament concluded that "therefore, the exclusion of arbitration from the scope of the Regulation should be preserved…"[57]

The above facts lead to a position strongly against the harmonisation of international commercial arbitration in the EU, holding that "'communitarise' international arbitration would be useless and dangerous".[58] It is feared that such harmonisation "would affect the right of each Member State to shape its arbitration laws as it deems proper so as to better meet the needs of the business community and attract arbitration within its form".[59]

However, this argument ignores the fact that EU legislation has already inevitably influenced more or less the domestic legal system, including arbitration. The reasons are within the process of the EU's targets and goals for European integration and the need to for establishment of a "European area of justice" for civil and commercial matters.[60] This article will argue that in order to build the internal market in the EU and the need to promote the EU as an arbitration-friendly region, harmonisation of interim measures, including the emergency arbitrator mechanism, is necessary.

4.3.2 The Need to Build the Internal Market

The foundation of the legal harmonisation in the EU level is based on "a sufficient common core or a sufficient set of shared values"[61] despite the existing diversity in

[57] European Parliament's Committee on Legal Affairs 2012, Explanatory Statement, para 4.

[58] Benedettelli 2011, p. 583.

[59] Ibid.

[60] Ibid., p 585.

[61] Pfeiffer 2014, p. 206.

legal and cultural traditions in Member States. The difference in EU Member States' national laws could be an obstacle to the "sound operation of the internal market",[62] and may create unpredictability in parallel dispute resolution proceedings and conflicting results.[63]

As an important forum to solve the commercial disputes, arbitration may be one of the best ways to "initiate a bottom-up influence on the harmonisation of procedural rules".[64] Due to the fundamental principle—party autonomy, parties are given the right to determine the procedural rules and the laws governing the merits, and arbitrators have a broader discretion than judges to apply the law and commercial practice. Additionally, the arbitrators and councils from different legal systems and cultures increase the blending and improvement of laws.

The European Commission, in its 2009 Green Paper on the review of the Brussels I Regulation No 44/2001, emphasized that the address to certain aspects is not meant to regulate arbitration, but "in the first place to ensure the smooth circulation of judgments in Europe and prevent parallel proceedings".[65] Article 81 of the Treaty on the Function of the European Union (TFEU) states the principle of mutual recognition to develop the judicial cooperation among Member States and the European Parliament and the Council shall adopt measures in need of the internal market. Such principle applies not only to judgments but also to "decisions in extrajudicial cases"[66] which "can well be construed as referring also to arbitral awards."[67]

Therefore, arbitration should be seen as a necessary part of civil and commercial judicial cooperation in Member States and should be subject to EU law as well.

4.3.3 Promoting the EU as an Arbitration-Friendly Region

International commercial arbitration is an irreplaceable, preferred dispute resolution worldwide,[68] but also a tool to create an arbitration-friendly region for the economic growth and globalisation.[69] Lacking uniform and harmonized rules governing the interim measures granted by the emergency arbitrator raises legal uncertainty in arbitration.

---

[62] Council Regulation (EC) No 44/2001 of 22 December 2000 on Jurisdiction and the recognition and enforcement of judgments in civil and commercial matters (Brussels I), Recital (2).

[63] Benedettelli 2011, p. 599.

[64] Pfeiffer 2014, p. 206.

[65] Commission of the European Communities 2009, Sect. 7; Gaffney 2017, p. 92.

[66] Treaty on the Functioning of the European Union, Article 81(2)(b).

[67] Benedettelli 2011, p. 599.

[68] Queen Mary University of London and White & Case LLP 2015, p. 2.

[69] McConnaughay 2013, p. 9.

Traditionally arbitration is welcomed in Europe in history due to the fact that commercial arbitration can be traced back to the ancient Greece period.[70] However, things become to change in the current age owing to high levels of globalisation and rapid growth of international transactions.

According to the 2015 International Arbitration Survey: Improvements and Innovations in International Arbitration, the five most preferred and widely used seats of arbitration were London, Paris, Hong Kong, Singapore and Geneva.[71] The preference of certain arbitral seats is influenced by the legal infrastructure of the seats, the neutrality and impartiality, the arbitration law and the record of enforcement.[72]

The arbitration law plays a key role in internationalization and modernization of international arbitration. The seats open to innovations and convenience tend to be welcomed by parties. The two Asian regions are the best examples. Regarding the emergency arbitrator mechanism, these two seats have both recently amended their arbitration laws in order to keep pace with the development of modern arbitration.

Singapore's 2012 International Arbitration Act, Interpretation of Part II 2(1) provides that 'arbitral tribunal' means a sole arbitration or a panel of arbitrators or a permanent arbitral institution, and includes an emergency arbitrator appointed pursuant to the rules of arbitration agreed to or adopted by the parties including the rules of arbitration of an institution or organization".[73] In Part II 12(6), it reads "[a]ll orders or directions made or given by an arbitral tribunal in the courts of an arbitration shall, by leave of the High Court or a Judge thereof, be enforceable in the same manner as if they were orders made by a court".[74] With the interpretation in Part II 2(1), the recognition and enforcement of interim measures granted by an emergency arbitrator in Singapore is without barriers.

Situations are similar in Hong Kong. The Amendments to the Arbitration Ordinance (Cap. 609) 2013 states that "[a]ny emergency relief granted, whether in or outside Hong Kong, by an emergency arbitrator under the relevant arbitration rules is enforceable in the same manner as an order or direction of the Court that has the same effect, but only with the leave of the Court"[75] in Article 22B(1). The new arbitration law in Hong Kong is regarded as probably the "most favourable regime for enforcement of emergency decisions".[76]

The acceptance of emergency arbitration mechanism in these two jurisdictions is not accidental, which indicates the openness and friendliness of arbitration in Singapore and Hong Kong. Unsurprisingly, with those changes, Singapore is

[70] Born 2014, p. 26.

[71] Queen Mary University of London and White & Case LLP 2015, p. 2.

[72] Ibid.

[73] Singapore International Arbitration Act 2012, Part II 2(1).

[74] Singapore International Arbitration Act 2012, Part II 12(6).

[75] Hong Kong Arbitration (Amendment) Bill 2013, Part 3A, Article 22B(1).

[76] Santacroce 2015, p. 310.

considered to be the most improved arbitral seat in the last five years, followed by Hong Kong.[77]

4.4 Possibility of Harmonisation in Arbitral Interim Measures in the EU

The harmonisation of emergency arbitrator mechanisms has the natural favourable position in the EU. Not only because the nature and status of the EU itself, but also for the previous efforts inside and outside of the European Union.

4.4.1 Previous Experience of Harmonisation of Arbitration in the EU

The uniformity and harmonisation of arbitration in the EU is not a total blank. There are two conventions regulating arbitration, namely the European Convention on International Commercial Arbitration 1961 and the European Convention providing a Uniform Law on Arbitration 1966.

The European Convention on International Commercial Arbitration 1961 with 18 EU Member States as contracting parties, which is "one of the world's most important regional commercial arbitration treaties".[78] This Convention was drafted by the United Nations Economic Commission for Europe during the cold war time, aimed to deal with the common problems of arbitral procedures among European countries, especially for the East and West of Europe.[79] The Convention "was the first international instrument to treat international commercial arbitration as a whole",[80] with provisions directly governing the stages of arbitral proceedings. The provisions do not cover the recognition and enforcement of arbitral awards, leaving those issues dealt with by other conventions including the New York Convention.

In practice, the European Convention on International Commercial Arbitration 1961 "never really achieved real international recognition."[81] The impact of the Convention has been "modest"[82] owing to the limited contracting parties are all members of the New York Convention. However, the Convention's efforts on international arbitration doctrines are highly significant, for example the

[77] Queen Mary University of London and White & Case LLP 2015, p. 2.

[78] Born 2014, p. 117.

[79] Redfern et al. 2004, p. 460.

[80] Fouchard et al. 1999, p. 140.

[81] Lew et al. 2003, p. 23.

[82] Born 2015, Sect. 1.04.

competence-competence principle and party autonomy.[83] As time passes by, the Convention is "currently somewhat dated",[84] new adjustments are needed.

Another one is the European Convention providing a Uniform Law on Arbitration 1966, which has only been signed by Austria and Belgium. Belgium is the only one of the two signatories to ratify the Convention. This Convention is designed to provide for a uniform national and international arbitration law and for "more effective settlement of private law disputes by arbitration in international relations"[85] by the Council of Europe. Unfortunately, it has never come into force,[86] and "is unlikely to do so".[87]

4.4.2 *Worldwide Harmonisation Experiences in Arbitration*

The United Nations Commission on International Trade Law (UNCITRAL) is the "core legal body of the United Nations system in the field of international trade law".[88] The goal of UNCITRAL is the "modernization and harmonisation of rules on international business".[89] As a UN based body, UNCITRAL has done plenty efforts in promoting "modern, fair, and harmonized rules on commercial transactions",[90] for example, the United Nations Convention on Contracts for the International Sale of Goods (CISG), and its UNCITRAL Model Law on cross-border insolvency, international payments and other various international legal fields.

Among the efforts of UNCITRAL, there are two documents concerned with interim measures in international commercial arbitration discussed in this article—the Convention on the Recognition and Enforcement of Foreign Arbitral Awards 1958 (New York Convention) and the UNCITRAL Model Law on International Commercial Arbitration 2006 (UNCITRAL Model Law).

4.4.2.1 The New York Convention

The Convention on the Recognition and Enforcement of Foreign Arbitral Awards 1958 (New York Convention) is a milestone in international arbitration.

---

[83] Born 2014, p. 118; European Convention on International Commercial Arbitration 1961, Article IV and Annex.

[84] Born 2014, p. 119.

[85] Gaffney 2017, p. 85.

[86] Lew et al. 2003, p. 23.

[87] Fouchard et al. 1999, p. 145.

[88] UNCITRAL 2017a, para 1.

[89] Ibid.

[90] Ibid., para 2.

Although it is a remarkably short treaty with only 16 articles, it has become the foundation of prosperity of international arbitration and a "rampart of the security of international contracts".[91] The two focus points of the Convention—insuring the arbitral agreement to be respected, and the arbitral awards to be recognized and enforced, are served very well. As Sudan acceded to the New York Convention on 26 March 2018, there are 159 contracting parties so far, including most major business states in the world. It is noted that all EU Member States have signed the said convention.

The New York Convention was drafted in order to "provide common legislative standards for recognition of arbitration agreements and court recognition and enforcement of foreign and non-domestic arbitral awards".[92] A broader goal of the Convention is to encourage the international commerce by adopting an efficient and neutral procedural rule for dispute resolution.[93]

Notwithstanding its success in promoting international arbitration, there is no provision stating the recognition and enforcement of interim measures by the arbitral tribunal, not to mention the decision by the emergency arbitrator. It is highly controversial whether the interim measures can be regarded as arbitral awards, since there is a "finality" requirement in the preparing and drafting history.[94] However, this element has been deleted in the official text of the Convention. The uncertainty in the interpretation of the wording leads to unpredictability and uncertainty for the recognition and enforcement of interim measures by the emergency arbitrator leaves the possible future solutions in this field.

4.4.2.2 The UNCITRAL Model Law

The UNCITRAL Model Law on International Commercial Arbitration (1985) with the amendments as adopted in 2006 aims "to assist States in reforming and modernizing their laws on arbitral procedure"[95] taking the needs of international commercial arbitration into account. So far, 80 States of a total of 111 jurisdictions have adopted the UNCITRAL Model Law, of which 31 jurisdictions have adopted the 2006 amendments.[96] 18 EU Member States introduced the UNCITRAL Model

[91] Paulsson 2016, p. 1.

[92] Convention on the Recognition and Enforcement of Foreign Arbitral Awards 1958 (New York Convention), Introduction.

[93] Paulsson 2016, p. 1.

[94] Geneva Convention on the Execution of Foreign Arbitral Awards 1927, Article 1(d) and Article 4.

[95] UNCITRAL 2017b, para 1.

[96] UNCITRAL 2018, para 3.

Law into the domestic legal framework, with Belgium, Ireland, Lithuania, and Slovenia adopting the 2006 version.

In the previous UNCITRAL Model Law 1985, there is an Article 17 granting the arbitral tribunal the power to order interim measures. In the 2006 amendments, the Article has been developed into a chapter (Chapter IV A. Interim Measures and Preliminary Orders). As explained by the Secretary General, UNCITRAL's focus on interim measures reflects the increasing number of cases seeking interim measures and the lack of certain uniformed guidance of interim measures in practice.[97]

Article 17 of the UNCITRAL Model Law 2006 regulates three essential elements in arbitral interim measures. Firstly, the scope and categories of interim measures could be granted by the arbitral tribunal.[98] Secondly, the standards for the arbitral tribunals to issue the requested interim measures.[99] Thirdly, the recognition and enforcement of arbitral tribunal granted interim measures in state courts and the grounds for refusal.[100] Lastly, the same concurrent power of state courts issues the interim measures based on their own procedural laws with the features of international commercial arbitration.[101]

The UNCITRAL supports the idea that it would be a huge significant step if the provisions dealing with the procedure for the enforcement of interim measures can be uniformed.[102] With all the improvements compared to the previous version of UNCITRAL Model Law, due to the limits of the historical background when the amendments were made, there is no provision concerning the emergency arbitrator mechanism. However, future harmonisation of emergency arbitrator mechanisms can borrow the framework of the UNCITRAL Model Law 2006 with regard to the interim measures.

4.4.3 Suggestion

After the judgment of *Allianz v. West Tankers*[103] in the European Court of Justice, the Brussels I Regulation Recast adopted an approach that the arbitration proceedings are excluded from the application, and the scope is identified.[104] However, this could raise serious conflicts among Member State courts, and interaction

[97] UNCITRAL Working Group on Arbitration 2000a, para 104.

[98] UNCITRAL Model Law on International Commercial Arbitration 2006, Article 17.

[99] UNCITRAL Model Law on International Commercial Arbitration 2006, Article 17A.

[100] Article 17 H and I, UNCITRAL Model Law on International Commercial Arbitration 2006, Article 17H and I.

[101] UNCITRAL Model Law on International Commercial Arbitration 2006, Article 9 and 17J.

[102] Bucy 2010, p. 603.

[103] CJEU Case C-185/07 *Allianz v. West Tankers* [2009] E.C.R. I-663.

[104] Regulation (EU) No 1215/2012 of the European Parliament and the Council of 12 December 2012 on jurisdiction and recognition and enforcement of judgments in civil and commercial matters (Recast)(Brussels I Recast), Recital 12.

between arbitral tribunals and state courts. Additionally, even though there are international conventions governing the arbitration, for example the New York Convention enjoying a higher hierarchy,[105] these conventions only cover a limited range of issues in the arbitral proceedings. Particularly regarding interim measures including the emergency arbitrator mechanism, there is no existing uniform regulation.

Such potential conflicts between EU law and Member States' arbitration law "need to be reconciled under a more consistent single framework".[106] Meanwhile, it shall be kept in mind that the EU harmonisation in arbitration should have the link to the goals of European integration.[107] In order to do so, three basic principles which are valued by the EU and Member States should be respected, namely "conferral", "subsidiarity", and "proportionality".[108] The principle of conferral limits the competence of EU within the powers granted by the Member States. The principle of subsidiarity guides the EU to exercise the power to achieve the objectives that cannot be better done by the Member States. The principle of proportionality requires the EU to act when necessary.

Taking into the above analysis and consideration, this article proposed that the EU needs a set of unified rules with regard to arbitration in the field of interim measures. An Emergency arbitrator mechanism is a good point to start with. The harmonisation of emergency arbitrator mechanisms should play the role as a supplement of the New York Convention and the UNCITRAL Model Law, under which the emergency arbitrator mechanism is not regulated, and to be minimalist based on the principles above. Of course, the balance between the EU and its Member States and the private parties involved in international transactions, shall be carefully determined.[109]

To achieve the final objective, the first step is to encourage the Member States to adopt the UNCITRAL Model Law or a similar approach. Then, further harmonisation will be achieved with the future "duplicative action" at the EU level and the New York Convention.[110]

4.5 Conclusion

The increasing importance of interim measures granted by the emergency arbitration catches the eyes from the international commercial arbitration community, as well as the international investment arbitration experts. Contrary to rapid

---

[105] Ibid.

[106] Benedettelli 2011, p. 598.

[107] Ibid.

[108] Treaty on the European Union, Article 5.

[109] Gaffney 2017, p. 96.

[110] Ibid., p. 98.

development in arbitral institutional rules, fewer national arbitration laws regulate the emergency arbitrator procedures, which leads to a serious problem of recognition and enforcement. Especially in the context of the EU, in which internal market and judicial mutual trust are rooted. Therefore, a harmonized emergency arbitrator mechanism is necessary. Beside the necessity, the previous experiences in both EU and from UN could be used as reference in order to make a leading pioneer in unifying the provisions for interim measures granted by the emergency arbitrator.

After all, the problem about "when" and "how" should the EU law regulating the matters concerning the emergency arbitrator mechanism cannot be answered with a fast and short answer. This article aims to enlighten scholars and future discussion for promoting the international commercial arbitration, and in the end, the international trade.

References

Athhan Ö (2011) The Main Principle Governing Interim Measures in the Pre-arbitral Proceedings —Specifically, the ICC Emergency Arbitrator Rules (2012). Annales de la Faculté de Droit d'Istanbul, 43:203–262

Benedettelli MV (2011) "Communitarization" of International Arbitration: A New Spectre Haunting Europe? IntALR 27:583–622

Boog C (2013) Commentary on the ICC Rules, Article 29 [Emergency arbitrator]. In: Arroyo M (ed) Arbitration in Switzerland: The Practitioner's Guide. Kluwer Law International, The Netherlands, pp 814–825

Born GB (2014) International Commercial Arbitration. Kluwer Law International, The Netherlands

Born GB (2015) International Arbitration: Law and Practice. Kluwer Law International, The Netherlands

Bose R, Meredith I (2012) Emergency Arbitration Procedures: A Comparative Analysis. IntALR 15:186–194

Bucy DR (2010) How to Best Protect Party Rights: The Future of Interim Relief in International Commercial Arbitration under the Amended UNCITRAL Model Law. Am. U. Int'l L. Rev. 25:579–609

Commission of the European Communities (2009) Green Paper on the Review of Council Regulation (EC) No 44/2001 on jurisdiction and the recognition and enforcement of judgments in civil and commercial matters. http://eur-lex.europa.eu/legal-content/EN/TXT/?uri=celex:52009DC0175. Accessed 28 March 2017

European Parliament's Committee on Legal Affairs (2012) Report on the proposal for a regulation of the European Parliament and of the Council on jurisdiction and the recognition and enforcement of judgments in civil and commercial matters (Recast)(COM(2010) 0748-C7-0433/2010-2010/0383(COD)). http://www.europarl.europa.eu/sides/getDoc.do?pubRef=-//EP//TEXT+REPORT+A7-2012-0320+0+DOC+XML+V0//EN&language=ga#title2. Accessed 28 March 2017

European Parliament's Committee on Legal Affairs (2014) Legal Instruments and Practice of Arbitration in the EU. http://www.europarl.europa.eu/RegData/etudes/STUD/2015/509988/IPOL_STU(2015)509988_EN.pdf. Accessed 28 March 2017

European Union (2017) The EU in brief. https://europa.eu/european-union/about-eu/eu-in-brief_en. Accessed 28 March 2017

Fouchard P, Gaillard E, Goldman B, Savage J (1999) Fouchard and Gaillard Goldman on International Commercial Arbitration. Kluwer Law International, The Netherlands

Gaffney J (2017) Should the European Union regulate commercial arbitration? IntALR 33:81–98

Gaillard E, Pinsolle P (2004) The ICC Pre-Arbitral Referee: First Practical Experience. ArbIntl 20:13–37

ICC (2017) Arbitration. https://iccwbo.org/dispute-resolution-services/arbitration/. Accessed 30 March 2017

ICC (2018) ICC announces 2017 figures confirming global reach and leading position for complex, high-value disputes. https://iccwbo.org/media-wall/news-speeches/icc-announces-2017-figures-confirming-global-reach-leading-position-complex-high-value-disputes/. Accessed 1 June 2018

Kačevska I (2014) The European, Middle Eastern and African Arbitration Review, Latvia. http://globalarbitrationreview.com/insight/the-european-middle-eastern-and-african-arbitration-review-2015/1036882/latvia. Accessed 30 March 2017

LCIA (2014) Registrar's Report 2014. http://www.lcia.org/LCIA/reports.aspx. Accessed 30 March 2017

LCIA (2015) Registrar's Report 2015. http://www.lcia.org/LCIA/reports.aspx. Accessed 30 March 2017

LCIA (2016) Facts and Figures - 2016: A Robust Caseload. http://www.lcia.org/LCIA/reports.aspx. Accessed 1 June 2018

LCIA (2017) Facts and Figures - 2017 Casework Report. http://www.lcia.org/LCIA/reports.aspx. Accessed 1 June 2018

Lemenez G, Quigley P (2008) The ICDR's Emergency Arbitrator Procedure in Action. https://www.icdr.org/icdr/ShowPDF?doc=ADRSTG_004356. Accessed 28 March 2017

Lew JDM, Mistelis LA, Kröll SM (2003) Comparative International Commercial Arbitration. Kluwer Law International, The Netherlands

McConnaughay PJ (2013) The Role of Arbitration in Economic Development and the Creation of Transnational Legal Principles. http://www.pkusz.edu.cn/uploadfile/2013/1008/20131008051334815.pdf. Accessed March 2017

Mohmeded SSM (2016) The Enforcement of Provisional Measures by Tribunals and Courts in England. IAJLS 1:44–58

Moses M (2012) The Principles and Practice of International Commercial Arbitration. Cambridge University Press, New York

Paulsson MRP (2016) The 1958 New York Convention in Action. Kluwer Law International, The Netherlands

Pfeiffer T (2014) The Contribution of Arbitration to the Harmonisation of Procedural Laws in Europe. UniflRev 19:199–217

Queen Mary University of London, White & Case LLP (2012) 2012 International Arbitration Survey: Current and Preferred Practices in the Arbitral Process. http://www.arbitration.qmul.ac.uk/docs/164483.pdf. Accessed 28 March 2017

Queen Mary University of London, White & Case LLP (2015) 2015 International Arbitration Survey: Improvements and Innovations in International Arbitration. http://www.arbitration.qmul.ac.uk/docs/164761.pdf. Accessed 28 March 2017

Redfern A, Hunter M, Blackaby N, Partasides C (2004) Law and Practice of International Commercial Arbitration. Sweet & Maxwell, London

Santacroce FG (2015) The emergency arbitrator: a full-fledged arbitrator rendering an enforceable decision? ArbIntl 31:283–312

Savola M (2015) Interim Measures and Emergency Arbitrator Proceedings, Presentation at the 23rd Croatian Arbitration Days: Access to Arbitral Justice. http://arbitration.fi/files/2016/04/23-cad-savola-interim-measures-and-emergency-arbitrator-proceedings.pdf. Accessed 28 March 2017

SCC (2016) SCC Statistics 2015. http://sccinstitute.com/media/181705/scc-statistics-2015.pdf. Accessed 28 March 2017

SCC (2017) SCC Statistics 2016. http://sccinstitute.com/statistics/. Accessed 28 March 2017

SCC (2018) SCC Statistics 2017. http://sccinstitute.com/statistics/. Accessed 1 June 2018

Smith G (2016) The Emergence of Emergency Arbitrations. http://www.gordonsmithlegal.com.au/resources/Emergency%20Arbitrations%20(12082016).pdf. Accessed 29 March 2017

UNCITRAL Working Group on Arbitration (2000a) Possible uniform rules on certain issues concerning settlement of commercial disputes: conciliation, interim measures of protection, written form for arbitration agreement, Report of the Secretary General. https://documents-dds-ny.un.org/doc/UNDOC/LTD/V00/501/85/PDF/V0050185.pdf?OpenElement. Accessed 28 March 2017

UNCITRAL Working Group on Arbitration (2000b) Possible Future Work: Court-Ordered Interim Measures of Protection in Support of Arbitration, Scope of Interim Measures that May be Issued by Arbitral Tribunals, Validity of the Agreement to Arbitrate, Report of the Secretary General. https://documents-dds-ny.un.org/doc/UNDOC/LTD/V00/580/10/PDF/V0058010.pdf?OpenElement. Accessed 28 March 2017

UNCITRAL (2017a) About UNCITRAL. http://www.uncitral.org/uncitral/en/about_us.html. Accessed 28 March 2017

UNCITRAL (2017b) UNCITRAL Model Law on International Commercial. Arbitration (1985), with amendments as adopted in 2006 http://www.uncitral.org/uncitral/en/uncitral_texts/arbitration/1985Model_arbitration.html. Accessed 28 March 2017

UNCITRAL (2018) Status of UNCITRAL Model Law on International Commercial Arbitration (1985), with amendments as adopted in 2006. http://www.uncitral.org/uncitral/en/uncitral_texts/arbitration/1985Model_arbitration_status.html. Accessed 1 June 2018

Van Haersolte-Van Hof JJ (2014) Revision of the Dutch Arbitration Act: Making The Netherlands an Even Better Place for Arbitration. JIntlArb 31:425–437

Yesilirmark A (2005) Provisional Measures in International Commercial Arbitration. Kluwer Law International, The Netherlands

Chapter 5
Resolving Foreign Direct Investment-Related Disputes in China's Legal System: What to Expect and How to Understand?

Chunlei Zhao

Contents

Chunlei Zhao is working at Maastricht University, Maastricht, The Netherlands, as a Ph.D candidate. She studied in China at the EU School of Law from 2012 until 2015. She is working on a Ph.D thesis regarding the dispute settlement mechanism in the prospective China-EU Bilateral Investment Treaty and can be contacted via e-mail at chunlei_zhao@yahoo.com. The present work may constitute part of the author's Ph.D. thesis in the future.

C. Zhao (✉)
Maastricht University, Maastricht, The Netherlands
e-mail: chunlei_zhao@yahoo.com

V. Lazić and S. Stuij (eds.), *International Dispute Resolution*,
Short Studies in Private International Law,
https://doi.org/10.1007/978-94-6265-252-1_5

Abstract In the past decade, China has become one of the most popular destinations for foreign direct investment in the world. For resolving disputes arising from investment in China, dispute settlement mechanisms in China's domestic legal system are indispensable. This paper offers an overview of the current domestic dispute settlement mechanisms in China's legal system for foreign direct investment-related disputes. These mechanisms include negotiation, mediation, arbitration, complaints coordination for foreign investment, administrative review and litigation. The design of each mechanism and the features of the whole dispute resolution system resonate with the virtues presented in Chinese ideology under the influence of traditional philosophies. Therefore, it is meaningful to explore the connection between the features of these mechanisms and Chinese ideology, in order to better understand the underlying values that they intend to protect. At the same time, because of China's successful operation, it is speculated that its domestic dispute settlement mechanisms for foreign direct investment-related disputes would likely have an influence on other jurisdictions in the world, which can take advantage of China's experience but may also need to take their own legal ideologies into consideration.

Keywords: Amicable settlement · China's legal system · dispute settlement mechanism · foreign direct investment · ideology · traditional philosophy

5.1 Introduction

For resolving foreign direct investment-related disputes,[1] compared to international arbitration, the dispute settlement mechanisms (hereinafter "DSMs") within a host state's domestic legal system are convenient to access, relatively cheaper and better for subsequent operation of the investment after the dispute resolution process. In addition, international arbitration is not available under all investment agreements; even when investment arbitration is provided for by the disputed investment agreement, exhausting domestic resorts may be explicitly required.[2]

In the past decade, China has become one of the most popular destinations of foreign direct investment in the world. According to the World Investment Reports issued by the United Nations Conference on Trade and Development (UNCTAD), China was one of the three largest recipients of foreign direct investment

[1] The phrase "FDI-related disputes" used in the present work refers to the legal disputes that may happen during foreign direct investment. Based on the nature of disputing parties, these disputes can be divided into two categories: first, disputes between foreign investors and the government of the host state; second, disputes between foreign investors and merchants of the host state.

[2] See e.g. Agreement between the Belgium-Luxembourg Economic Union and the Government of the People's Republic of China on the Reciprocal Promotion and Protection of Investment, Article 8.2: "...It's mutually understood that the People's Republic of China requires that the investor concerned *exhausts the domestic administrative review procedure* specified by the laws and regulations of the People's Republic of China, before submission of the dispute to international arbitration under Article 8, para 2...[emphasis added]."

(hereinafter "FDI") in the past three years.[3] Regarding resolving FDI-related disputes in China's domestic legal system, there are multiple DSMs. Each mechanism has its own features, and at the same time, they constitute a broad picture of China's legal system for FDI-related dispute resolution. This system is branded with Chinese characteristics, the root of which can be traced back to influential traditional Chinese philosophies.

The present work aims at providing a general picture of China's domestic DSMs for FDI-related disputes and interpreting these mechanisms from a Chinese ideological perspective. This paper will initially provide an overview of the DSMs in China's legal system, including negotiation, mediation, arbitration, complaints coordination for foreign investment, administrative review and litigation. After that, it explores the underlying values of these mechanisms, trying to understand this system in the context of Chinese ideology. The fourth section focuses on the potential influence of China's domestic DSMs for FDI-related disputes in the world and whether, and if so, how other countries can take advantage of China's experience.

5.2 Dispute Settlement Mechanisms for FDI-Related Disputes in China's Legal System

In terms of the DSMs provided by one's domestic legal system for resolving FDI-related disputes, like in many other countries, mediation, arbitration and litigation are available in China's current legal system. At the same time, negotiation is required by Chinese legal texts as a compulsory step for resolving certain kinds of disputes, so it is also seen as a part of the DSMs under Chinese laws by this section. Furthermore, with regard to disputes between private parties and administrative organs, another two mechanisms have been established, which are complaints coordination for foreign investment and administrative reconsideration. Thus, there are six DSMs in China's legal system for resolving FDI-related disputes, the basic structure and features of which are introduced as follows.

5.2.1 Negotiation

Negotiation often refers to the process of discussing the dispute with the other disputing party in order to reach a mutually acceptable solution without any

---

[3] China was the third-largest recipient of foreign direct investment in 2015, the first largest in 2014 and the second largest in 2013. See: United Nations Conference on Trade and Development (UNCTAD) 2016, p. 5; United Nations Conference on Trade and Development (UNCTAD) 2015, p. 5.

intervention from a third party. As an informal DSM, negotiation is usually not regulated in laws; however, it has been particularly mentioned in Chinese legal texts from two aspects. First, negotiation is required as a prerequisite for resorting to other DSMs for certain kinds of disputes. For instance, the General Principles of the Civil Law of the People's Republic of China (2009) provides that, if there is any unclear provision in a contract, contracting parties are required to negotiate informally before bringing a case in front of a people's court.[4] Second, Chinese procedural laws often explicitly stress that negotiation is available to parties throughout the entire process of formal DSMs. For example, according to Civil Procedure Law of the People's Republic of China (2012), in litigation, unless the enforcement is completed, parties can reach a settlement through negotiation at any time.[5]

In summary, within China's legal system, negotiation is recommended, even required, to be conducted before or during any stage of formal DSMs. It can be said that these clear expressions in legal texts show a negotiation-friendly attitude of China's legal system.

5.2.2 Mediation

Mediation is another unstructured amicable DSM, where the settlement agreement, if possible, is reached with the assistance of a third neutral party as the mediator. Mediation has played a significant role in China's legal system for resolving disputes, including FDI-related ones, a particular reflection of which is its various positions in the whole dispute settlement system. Initially, mediation can be hosted by a commercial mediation commission.[6] Secondly, administrative mediation is offered by the State Administration of Industry and Commerce by using its

---

[4] General Principles of the Civil Law of the People's Republic of China (enforced on 1 January 1987, as amended on 27 August 2009), Article 88. Another example is the situation where there is a dispute over jurisdiction between people's courts. Such a dispute shall be resolved by the disputing parties through negotiation; if the negotiation fails, then the disputing courts can request their common superior people's court to specify the jurisdiction. See: Civil Procedure Law of the People's Republic of China (enforced on 9 April 1991, as amended on 31 August 2012), Article 37.

[5] Civil Procedure Law of the People's Republic of China (enforced on 9 April 1991, as amended on 31 August 2012), Articles 50, 230.

[6] In theory, this type of mediation can also be hosted by people's mediation commissions. However, in practice, people's mediation commissions are rarely used for resolving FDI-related disputes. Therefore, this section only focuses on mediation conducted by commercial mediation commissions.

branches as mediators for resolving disputes between economic organizations.[7] Thirdly, mediation can be a part of administrative reconsideration. Fourthly, mediation is conducted during the arbitration process, which is known as the "Arb-Med" or "Oriental Experience".[8] Finally, mediation is combined with litigation proceedings. All of these are briefly introduced in this section.

5.2.2.1 Independent Mediation Conducted by Commercial Mediation Commissions

In general, mediation conducted by commercial mediation commissions follows the principles of voluntariness and confidentiality.[9] If a settlement agreement is reached through mediation, the mediator will deliver a mediation statement. Such a statement constitutes a new contract between parties.[10] In particular, under the current Mediation Rules of the first and largest professional mediation organization in China, the China Council for the Promotion of International Trade (CCPIT)/China Chamber of International Commerce (CCOIC) Conciliation Centre, parties are provided with several options to ensure the compliance of such a new contract: first, parties may make an application to the competent people's court to confirm their settlement agreement;[11] second, if the settlement agreement only involves payment of debts, parties could apply to the competent people's court to issue an enforceable payment warrant;[12] third, parties could choose to have their settlement agreement notarized;[13] finally, it is also possible to transfer the case to the China International Economic and Trade Arbitration Commission (CIETAC) to conduct the arbitration procedures expeditiously and to get an arbitral award following the content of the settlement agreement.[14]

---

[7] The phrase "economic organizations" is defined as "legal person, individual partnerships, individual industrial and commercial households, lease-holding farm households and other economic organizations". (unofficial translation of

"法人、个人合伙、个体工商户、农村承包经营户以及其他经济组织")

See: Administration of Administrative Mediation of Contract Dispute by the State Administration for Industry and Commerce of the People's Republic of China (enforced on 3 November 1997), Article 6.

[8] Sussman 2009, pp. 71–74.

[9] CCPIT/CCOIC Mediation Rules (enforced on 1 May 2012), Article 4.

[10] Several Opinions of the Supreme People's Court on Establishing a Sound Conflict and Dispute Resolution Mechanism that Connects Litigation and Non-litigation, 24 July 2009.

[11] CCPIT/CCOIC Mediation Rules (enforced on 1 May 2012), Article 26.

[12] Ibid., Article 27. See also Civil Procedure Law of the People's Republic of China (enforced on 9 April 1991, as amended on 31 August 2012), Articles 214–217.

[13] CCPIT/CCOIC Mediation Rules (enforced on 1 May 2012), Article 27. See also: Notary Law of the People's Republic of China (enforced on 1 March 2006, as amended on 24 April 2015), Article 37.

[14] CCPIT/CCOIC Mediation Rules (enforced on 1 May 2012), Article 28.

5.2.2.2 Independent Mediation Conducted by Administrative Organs

The Administrative Mediation Rules for Contractual Disputes issued by the State Administration of Industry and Commerce of China on 3 November 1997 established administrative mediation, which is used as a mechanism "to maintain social and economic order".[15] The prerequisite of initiating this kind of mediation is that the dispute is a contractual dispute between economic organizations and has not been brought to a court or an arbitration commission.[16] Administrative organs, which usually are industry and commerce administrative authorities, mediate such disputes based on consent of disputing parties.[17] The process is not open to the public,[18] and it can be terminated at any time with one party's request.[19] If the dispute is successfully resolved through administrative mediation, disputing parties shall sign a mediation agreement or a new contract.[20] After that, like the mediation agreement reached in commercial mediation, parties can bring their new agreement to the competent people's court or a notarial institution to have it recognized or notarized. In fact, some branches of the State Administration of Industry and Commerce have established cooperation to connect administrative mediation with judicial confirmation from people's courts to facilitate disputing parties in confirming the result of administrative mediation.[21]

5.2.2.3 Mediation in Administrative Reconsideration

Administrative reconsideration applies to the situation where a citizen, a legal person or any other organization considers that his or its lawful rights and interests have been infringed upon by a specific administrative act and applies for administrative reconsideration to an administrative organ.[22] According to the Regulation on the Implementation of the Administrative Reconsideration Law of the People's Republic of China (2007), an administrative reconsideration organ may conduct mediation during the process of administrative reconsideration under the principles

---

[15] Administration of Administrative Mediation of Contract Dispute by the State Administration for Industry and Commerce of the People's Republic of China (enforced on 3 November 1997), Article 1.

[16] Ibid., Article 8.

[17] Ibid., Articles 2, 3, 8.

[18] Ibid., Article 5.

[19] Ibid., Article 17.

[20] Ibid., Articles 19.

[21] Wang 2012.

[22] Administrative Reconsideration Law of the People's Republic of China (enforced on 1 October 1999, as amended on 27 August 2009), Article 2. For further information of administrative reconsideration, see Sect. 5.2.5 of the present work.

of voluntariness and legality.[23] Where the parties concerned reach an agreement after mediation, the administrative reconsideration organ shall make a written Administrative Reconsideration Mediation Agreement.[24] Such a mediation agreement shall take effect in law upon being signed by both parties concerned and can be enforced by the competent administrative organs or by people's courts.[25]

5.2.2.4 Mediation in Arbitration

Mediation in arbitration is a special arrangement in the arbitration process, which combines mediation and arbitration through conducting mediation during the arbitration process whenever there is consent from parties. It has received high satisfaction from its Chinese customers.[26] This kind of mediation was created under the deep influence of the practices of conducting mediation in litigation in people's courts[27] and it has been expressly confirmed by the Arbitration Law of the People's Republic of China (2009).[28]

According to the Arbitration Law of the People's Republic of China (2009), a tribunal shall carry out mediation prior to delivering an arbitration award if both parties voluntarily refer to it.[29] In general, there is no clear distinction made between mediation phases and arbitration phases.[30] If the mediation successfully ends in a settlement agreement, disputing parties may withdraw their claim or counterclaim, or request the arbitral tribunal to render a written mediation statement or an arbitral award in accordance with the content of their settlement agreement.[31] The written mediation statement and the arbitral award have the same legal effect.[32]

[23] Regulation on the Implementation of the Administrative Reconsideration Law of the People's Republic of China (enforced on 1 August 2007), Article 50.

[24] Ibid.

[25] Ibid.

[26] Wang 2001, pp. 81–82.

[27] Kaufmann-Kohler and Kun 2008, p. 485.

[28] Arbitration Law of the People's Republic of China (enforced on 1 September 1995, as amended on 27 August 2009), Articles 51, 52.

[29] Ibid., Article 51.

[30] This is different from the practices in other mediation-friendly countries. For example, in South Korea and Indonesia, an arbitrator only attempts to mediate at the outset of arbitration and an arbitrator will suspend the arbitration if the parties agree to mediation during the course of arbitral proceedings. See: Scott 1995, p. 74.

[31] CIETAC Arbitration Rules (2015), Article 47.5.

[32] Arbitration Law of the People's Republic of China (enforced on 1 September 1995, as amended on 27 August 2009), Article 51. The differences between a mediation statement and an arbitral award based on the settlement agreement exists in the time point when the relevant document becomes effective. The written mediation statement shall become legally effective after both parties have signed for receipt thereof, while the award shall be legally effective as of the date on which it is made. See: Arbitration Law of the People's Republic of China (enforced on 1 September 1995, as amended on 27 August 2009), Articles 52, 57.

Where the disputing parties wish to mediate but hesitate to have the same tribunal acting as both arbitrators and mediators, it is possible to receive assistance from another independent mediator.[33]

5.2.2.5 Mediation in Litigation

Mediation in litigation has existed since the founding of the People's Republic of China. According to the Civil Procedure Law of the People's Republic of China (2012), during litigation, mediation can be referred to in three stages: before case registration,[34] after case registration but before a hearing and during or after a hearing but before the issuance of the final judgment. During the first stage, if parties reach an agreement, they could choose to apply to the competent people's court for issuance of a mediation agreement[35] or go to a notarial office to get their agreement notarized.[36] Without confirmation from people's courts or notarization, the settlement agreement has the same effect as a normal contract. If a consent statement is reached by disputing parties and issued by the people's court during the second stage, such a statement has the same effect of a judgment, which means one party can directly apply for enforcement if the other party does not follow it.[37] It is noticeable that such a consent statement cannot be appealed. If a party adduces enough evidence to prove that the conducted mediation violated the principle of voluntariness or the content of the consent statement violates laws, it may petition for a retrial.[38] If mediation fails, the court shall enter a judgment in a timely manner.[39] Finally, before the judgment is made, mediation could still be conducted to try to reach a settlement. The settlement agreement reached during this stage has similar effect to that of the one at the second stage.[40]

---

[33] CIETAC Arbitration Rules (2015), Article 47.8.

[34] The "case registration" here refers to the point when the people's court accepts the application made by the complainant and registers the case.

[35] Civil Procedure Law of the People's Republic of China (enforced on 9 April 1991, as amended on 31 August 2012), Articles 194–195.

[36] Notary Law of the People's Republic of China (enforced on 1 March 2006, as amended on 24 April 2015), Article 37.

[37] Civil Procedure Law of the People's Republic of China (enforced on 9 April 1991, as amended on 31 August 2012), Articles 97, 236.

[38] Ibid., Article 201.

[39] Ibid., Article 9.

[40] Ibid., Article 142.

5.2.3 Commercial Arbitration

China adopts a dual-track approach for arbitration and litigation, which treats domestic and foreign-related cases[41] separately. As a result, foreign-related arbitration cases are regulated by the provisions for domestic arbitration cases with necessary explicit amendments provided by laws. For serving the theme of the present work, this section only discusses the regulations on foreign-related arbitration cases.

According to the Arbitration Law of the People's Republic of China (2009), arbitration shall be carried out independently, free from interference of administrative organs, social organizations or individuals.[42] The precondition of referring a dispute to arbitration is having a valid arbitration agreement.[43] The challenge of the validity of an arbitration agreement may be submitted to the arbitration commission or the competent people's court. If one party requests the arbitration commission and the other party applies to the competent people's court for deciding on whether an arbitration agreement is valid or not, the people's court shall give a ruling.[44] This can be taken as the evidence that China does not completely recognize the doctrine of "competence-competence".[45] In foreign-related arbitration cases, parties are free to choose foreign arbitrators[46] and foreign lawyers are only prohibited from providing opinions in relation to the application of Chinese law.[47] Arbitration in China

[41] In Chinese law, a "foreign-related" case refers to a case where at least one of the following situations is satisfied: (1) either party or both parties are foreigners, stateless persons, foreign enterprises or organizations; (2) the habitual residence of either party or both parties is located outside the territory of China; (3) the subject matter is outside the territory of China; (4) the legal fact that leads to the establishment, change or termination of civil relationship occurs outside the territory of China; (5) any other circumstances under which a case may be determined as a foreign-related civil case. See: Interpretation of the Supreme People's Court on the Application of the Civil Procedure Law of the People's Republic of China (enforced on 4 February 2015), Article 522. Arbitration cases which satisfy this requirement are correspondingly referred to as "foreign-related arbitration" cases.

[42] Arbitration Law of the People's Republic of China (enforced on 1 September 1995, as amended on 27 August 2009), Article 8.

[43] According to the Arbitration Law of the People's Republic of China (2009), a valid arbitration agreement shall: "(1) be in written form; (2) contain an expression of intention to apply for arbitration, matters for arbitration, and a designated arbitration commission; (3) be within the range of arbitrable matters as specified by law". See: Arbitration Law of the People's Republic of China (enforced on 1 September 1995, as amended on 27 August 2009), Articles 3, 16, 17.

[44] Arbitration Law of the People's Republic of China (enforced on 1 September 1995, as amended on 27 August 2009), Article 20.

[45] The term "competence-competence" refers to the power/competence of an arbitral tribunal to decide upon its own jurisdiction/competence, which has been accepted as a basic doctrine in international arbitration. See: Hunter et al. 2015, para 5.105.

[46] Arbitration Law of the People's Republic of China (enforced on 1 September 1995, as amended on 27 August 2009), Article 67.

[47] Regulations on the Administration of Representative offices of foreign law firms in China (promulgated on 22 December 2001 and enforced on 1 January 2002), Article 15.

is held in camera, in principle. If the parties agree to make their arbitration public, the arbitration may be public unless state secrets are involved.[48] It is also noticeable that ad hoc arbitration is not allowed to be conducted in China.

5.2.4 Complaints Coordination for Foreign Investment

In 2006, the Ministry of Commerce of China promulgated the Interim Measures on Complaints from Foreign-invested Enterprises, according to which foreign-invested enterprises or foreign investors which deem that their legitimate rights or interests have been infringed by an administrative authority, may file a complaint with the complaint acceptance authority for coordination or settlement.[49]

In order to use this DSM, a dispute should not have entered into or gone through judicial procedures, administrative reconsideration, arbitral procedures, or have been accepted by the department of disciplinary inspection, supervision or credit investigation.[50] After receiving the complaint, the relevant organ will settle through administrative coordination, reflect the real situation, set forth suggestion, opinion or claim or transfer it to the local complaint acceptance organ or relevant department for handling.[51] This complaint coordination system is "quite flexible that foreign investors may resort to it either before or after the formal procedures".[52] In the recently published draft Foreign Investment Law of China, Article 118 clearly lists complaints coordination as one of the available DSMs for foreign investors to resolve the disputes within the territory of China, and provides relatively detailed guidance for using this newly created DSM.[53]

5.2.5 Administrative Reconsideration

Administrative reconsideration is another way of resolving potential disputes between investors and administrative authorities. In general, the process of the administrative reconsideration is similar to litigation, since administrative reconsideration organs enjoy likewise power as courts. According to the Administrative Reconsideration Law of the People's Republic of China (1999) and the Regulation

---

48 Arbitration Law of the People's Republic of China (enforced on 1 September 1995, as amended on 27 August 2009), Article 40.

49 Interim Measures of the Ministry of Commerce of the People's Republic of China for the Work Relating to the Complaints of Foreign-funded Enterprises (enforced on 1 October 2006), Article 2.

50 Ibid., Article 9.

51 Arbitration Law of the People's Republic of China (enforced on 1 September 1995, as amended on 27 August 2009), Articles 2, 11.

52 Wang 2011, p. 211.

53 Draft Foreign Investment Law (released on 19 January 2015), Chap. 8.

on the Implementation of Chinese Administrative Reconsideration Law (2007), the process of administrative reconsideration starts with the applicant's application for administrative reconsideration, in written form or in oral form, to the competent administrative organs.[54] After which, the respondent will reply in written form and provide the relevant documents to prove the basis of the specific administrative act that has been undertaken.[55] In principle, administrative reconsideration performs the examination based on the written submission, but if necessary, the administrative reconsideration organ may investigate facts amongst the organizations and citizens concerned and listen to the views of the applicant, respondent and third parties.[56] As a final step, the administrative reconsideration organ will make a decision, which can be enforced directly.[57] It is noted that party autonomy does not play as significant a role as it does in other DSMs. For example, although negotiation is also available in administrative reconsideration, it is the administrative organ that decides whether parties can withdraw the case or not if they reach a settlement agreement, which is similar to the situation in litigation.

5.2.6 Litigation

As mentioned above in Sect. 5.2.3, *supra*, China adopts a dual-track approach to differentiate the procedures for domestic and foreign-related litigation cases, which applies to both commercial litigation under the Civil Procedure Law of the People's Republic of China (2012) and administrative litigation under the Administrative Litigation Law of the People's Republic of China (2014).[58]

Regarding foreign-related commercial litigation under Chinese Civil Procedure Law (2012), there are some issues that deserve special attention.[59] First, litigation in people's courts adopts the principle of "counter-treatment" regarding procedural rights and obligations of foreign parties. Specifically, as a principle, foreign

[54] Administrative Reconsideration Law of the People's Republic of China (enforced on 1 October 1999, as amended on 27 August 2009), Articles 11–15.

[55] Ibid., Article 23.

[56] Draft Foreign Investment Law (released on 19 January 2015), Article 22. See also Regulation on the Implementation of the Administrative Reconsideration Law of the People's Republic of China (enforced on 1 August 2007), Articles 33–34.

[57] Administrative Reconsideration Law of the People's Republic of China (enforced on 1 October 1999, as amended on 27 August 2009), Articles 31–33. With regard to the enforcement of a decision from the administrative reconsideration process, there is no need to build any connection with the court system in order to rely on the power of people's courts. Administrative organs could use administrative power to force private parties to follow the decision or the effect of internal hierarchy to let the involved administrative organ change the disputed actions.

[58] Under Chinese law, litigation is further categorized as either civil litigation or administrative litigation.

[59] These points are either particularly designed for foreign-related cases, or exist with typical Chinese characteristics.

nationals, enterprises and organizations enjoy national treatment in people's courts. Where the courts of a foreign country impose any restrictions on the civil procedural rights of Chinese citizens, legal persons and other organizations, the people's courts shall apply the principle of reciprocity to the civil procedural rights of parties of that foreign country.[60] Second, as mentioned above in Sect. 5.2.5, *supra*, a plaintiff does not enjoy complete freedom on withdrawing its case, which could be the result of reaching an agreement with the defendant through negotiation. It is provided that where a plaintiff requests withdrawal of the action before a judgment is pronounced, the people's court shall issue a ruling regarding whether to grant such a request.[61] Third, if a foreign party needs to be represented by a lawyer as its agent *ad litem* in a people's court, a Chinese lawyer is the only choice.[62]

Administrative litigation happens where a foreign party refuses to accept the decision made by an administrative organ and brings a case in the competent people's court against that administrative organ.[63] The general procedure of administrative litigation is similar to the procedure for commercial litigation cases regulated by the Civil Procedure Law of the People's Republic of China (2012), with detailed differences to suit the specific nature of administrative disputes.

5.2.7 Summary

Although China's legal system comprises of various DSMs and each of them has its own features, it is clear that the whole system shows a strong preference to amicable resolution and in particular, China's firm belief that "conciliation represents the primary means to resolve transnational disputes while maintaining an ongoing business relationship".[64]

Particularly, mediation plays an inherent role in China's dispute resolution system. Although it is admitted that there are some questioning voices on the appropriateness of conducting mediation in other DSMs, the success of this "Oriental Experience" in China has proved its values and, at the same time, has drawn much attention from the world.[65] In fact, the preference for mediation has been explicitly pointed out by a Notice of "Giving Priority to Mediation, Combining Mediation with Judgment, Constructing the 'Triune' Big Mediation

---

[60] Civil Procedure Law of the People's Republic of China (enforced on 9 April 1991, as amended on 31 August 2012), Article 5.

[61] Ibid., Article 145.

[62] In terms of litigation in people's courts, foreign lawyers need to cooperate with Chinese lawyers and cannot provide opinions on the interpretation of Chinese legal documents. Civil Procedure Law of the People's Republic of China (enforced on 9 April 1991, as amended on 31 August 2012), Article 263.

[63] Hu 2003, p. 309.

[64] Farina 1989, p. 157.

[65] Chan 1997, p. 543. See also Stipanowich et al. 2009, pp. 379–414.

System of People's Mediation, Administrative Mediation and Judicial Mediation" issued by the Supreme People's Court in 2010.[66] It can be said that "Mediation First" has been established as a basic principle of dispute resolution in China's legal system, which reinforces the general preference to amicable DSMs. Besides mediation, other informal DSMs also play indispensable parts. As has been pointed out, "Chinese societies and legal arrangements over disputes point towards social patterns of dispute resolution rather than state-sponsored official fora".[67]

Although it has not been explicitly stated, it is reasonable to conclude that the basic tune of the design of China's dispute resolution system for FDI-related disputes is resolving disputes, instead of seeking justice. In other words, the purpose of establishing those DSMs is more about resolving disputes and restoring the relationship between disputing parties, instead of obtaining a decision on which party is right or wrong. This resonates with the values and teachings advocated by Chinese ideology under the influence of traditional Chinese philosophies. Thus, the next section explores the ideological foundation of China's dispute resolution system.

5.3 Interpreting China's DSMs for FDI-Related Disputes from the Perspective of Chinese Ideology

This section aims at exploring the potential connection between Chinese ideology under the influence of traditional philosophies and the features of the DSMs discussed in Sect. 5.5.2, *supra*. In order to do so, it first assesses the guidance for dispute resolution from Chinese ideology. After that, it explores the correspondence between the Chinese ideology and the DSMs in China's legal system, all with a mind to interpreting the DSMs from the perspective of Chinese ideology.

5.3.1 Guidance for Dispute Resolution from Chinese Ideology

There should be no doubt that the values and teachings from traditional Chinese philosophies, especially Confucianism, have exerted a significant effect on diverse aspects of Chinese legal tradition, and dispute resolution is a typical example.[68] This sub-section introduces the main relevant values and teachings from these

[66] Notice of the Supreme People's Court on Issuing Several Opinions on Further Implementing the Working Principle of "Giving Priority to Mediation and Combining Mediation with Judgment" (issued on 7 June 2010), Article 1.1.2.

[67] Meski 2009, p. 517.

[68] Bodde and Morris 1967, p. 5.

philosophies, after which it analyses whether, if so, how they have been inherited or changed by socialist morality, which is the ideology in contemporary China.

5.3.1.1 Guidance from Traditional Philosophies

Harmony First

A comprehensive harmony was promoted by traditional philosophies as the ultimate goal of a society. In other words, the permanent pursuance of harmony was placed on the top of various asserted values. This could be proved by, for example, the Analects by Confucius, which are the core texts of Confucianism. It is stated in the Analects that in the application of the rites, harmony is to be prized (礼之用和为贵). Harmony of the community enjoyed priority over other things and required every effort from each member of the society.[69] As a result, disputes were unpleasant disturbances, which were undesirable and should be avoided.

Relationship v. Justice

Harmony led to inculcated concurrent emphasis on maintaining good relationships among people.[70] Personal self-cultivation through "learning to become a responsible contributor to the completion of moral society"[71] was required in order to maintain an amicable relationship. The main purpose of interaction was establishing a conflict-free, interpersonal and social relationship, which related closely to relationship management. In essence, it was about avoiding disputes by managing to keep the relationship in a perfectly functional condition.

When disputes arose, people were encouraged to compromise, instead of seeking justice. In accordance with this line of thinking, harmonious relationships were more appreciated than individuals' rights and interests. "[B]alancing and harmonisation were considered more important than determining who was right and who was wrong."[72] Therefore, during the process of dispute resolution, accordingly, Chinese parties focused more on repairing the relationship, instead of arguing for their rights based on contractual provisions.

[69] Wang 2011, p. 222.

[70] Low 1996, p. 3.

[71] Ibid.

[72] Meski 2009, p. 557.

Informal Methods v. Formal Mechanisms

Since dispute resolution in China was a process of repairing relationships, win-win instead of win-lose oriented DSMs were recommended.[73] This was usually achieved through informal DSMs, such as negotiation and mediation. Using a formal mechanism for resolving disputes, such as litigation in a court, meant trouble and relationship failure. In ancient China, a court was a place connected with severe punishment instead of a forum for justice.[74] This could be taken as one of the reasons of the unpopularity of litigation in China.[75] Furthermore, Chinese society's resentment of litigation and courts was contributed by another two interrelated elements: first, a lawsuit itself was regarded as negative since it put individuals' interests over the overall benefits of society by breaking the order; second, a litigious society led to an unpleasant, uncomfortable and even unacceptable situation because it ran against the general pursuance of harmony. Therefore, resolving disputes through a lawsuit in a formal mechanism was deemed a lose-lose choice, and any form of litigious activity was "an indication of selfishness and as a threat to universal cosmic harmony".[76] Non-litigation methods are the preferred means and are better suited to the Chinese environment.

In summary, bringing a dispute to a formal DSM, or even just threatening with legal action, was never a good choice when dealing with disputes in China, since it would probably destroy the relationship between parties.

5.3.1.2 Guidance from Socialist Morality

In China's current ideology, teachings from traditional philosophies have been replaced by "Socialist Morality", but there is no dramatic deviation with regard to the core value. In fact, although the traditional guidance no longer acts as "binding" standards, most of which have been inherited explicitly or implicitly. One of the most prominent reflection is that the ultimate goal of socialist construction is defined as building a "socialist harmonious society",[77] which is a clear inheritance of the traditional pursuance of harmony. Furthermore, since harmony is still taken as the pinnacle of the society's value system, similarly, individuals are expected to self-discipline and submerge their interests for society to have a harmonious environment.

Compared to the value system from traditional philosophies, the Socialist value system elevates the status of law to a great extent; in fact, law has been taken as an indispensable part of the socialist construction to improve the state's legal system

[73] Fang 2006, p. 55.

[74] Pan 2011, p. 237.

[75] Bodde and Morris 1967, p. 6.

[76] Meski 2009, p. 547.

[77] Decision of the Central Committee of the Communist Party of China on Building Harmonious Society of Socialism (issued on 11 October 2006).

and to strengthen the public's legal consciousness. However, the emphasis on law is taken as one of the basic principles serving for building a socialist harmonious society.[78] In other words, the enhancement of the status of law is subject to the central theme of socialist harmony.[79]

5.3.2 Connection Between Chinese Ideology and the DSMs in China's Legal System

As part of Chinese ideology, the harmony-centred tradition greatly affected, if not dominated, patterns of dispute resolution in the past and still has tremendous influence on China's modern legal system, including the DSMs for FDI-related disputes therein.

First of all, the explicit reference to and encouragement of negotiation in Chinese legal texts and the great freedom given to disputing parties to use it, show the welcoming attitude towards negotiation. This informal DSM is beneficial to the re-establishment of a harmonious relationship between disputing parties and in line with the core value in Chinese ideology, the pursuance of social harmony.

Second, the great role played by mediation in China's legal system is probably accounted in part by the encouragement to use amicable means for resolving disputes in Chinese ideology. The basic principles and features of mediation are in line with the traditional values of Chinese society and in turn, it has the ability to help maintain harmonious relationships. In particular, China's creation of a combination of mediation with other DSMs typically shows China's intention to promote the use of mediation, which is probably contributed by the clear coherence between Chinese ideology and the underlying value of this kind of DSM. It can be said that the beliefs and philosophies from traditional Chinese philosophies have moulded China's legal system towards mediation in a great way.

Third, the design of China's whole dispute resolution system reflects an intended avoidance of using formal mechanisms, the origin of which can also be found in Chinese ideology. As has been pointed out by scholars, in particular, litigation in a court is not encouraged in both traditional and contemporary Chinese ideology.[80] The features of litigation, such as the adversarial methods used to sharpen parties' points of conflict and to stress their adversarial positions, as well as the enforcement on one party to accept the result of the decision, are in direct conflict with Chinese ideology.[81] In other words, avoiding adversarial posturing is in line with Chinese traditional values of maintaining relationships and loyalty for "old friends".[82]

---

[78] Ibid.

[79] Mo Zhang 2010, p. 42.

[80] Wang 2011, p. 209. See also George 1980, p. 68.

[81] George 1980, p. 68.

[82] Farina 1989, p. 158.

In brief, it is quite clear that the design of the DSMs for FDI-related disputes in China has been strongly influenced by Chinese ideology, as a result of which, amicable and informal mechanisms are taken as more honourable methods than confrontational ones.

5.4 The Influence of China's Domestic DSMs: Useful to the Development in Other Jurisdictions?

China's dispute resolution system for FDI-related disputes has formed its own characteristics. Such special, if not unique, practice regarding DSMs has drawn great attention from the world.[83] This comes not only from the perspective of foreign investors that need to take notice of the legal environment in the host state, but also from other states' points of view in terms of the design of their domestic dispute resolution systems.

On the one hand, China's experience illustrates the oriental understanding of dispute resolution and provides other jurisdictions with a potential option regarding the design of DSMs in a legal system. This system is established basically based on the pursuance of resolving disputes and maintaining relationships by greatly relying on "non-confrontational and less visible"[84] DSMs. Although formal DSMs are provided, where adjudication is conducted according to applicable laws, they are discouraged and unwelcomed. It is expected that with China's increasing role in international economics, particularly in the area of international investment, the influence of China's domestic DSMs for FDI-related disputes will be enhanced. In other words, the success of this "Chinese Model" may promote greater use of amicable DSMs in other jurisdictions.

As analysed above, the "Chinese Model" has its root in Chinese ideology, which raises the question how this special model could offer inspiration to other jurisdictions in the world. China's successful application proves that the DSMs in China's current legal system are useful for resolving disputes, especially in terms of their function of restoring the relationship between disputing parties. This is particularly important for any foreign investor that still expects further operation in the host state after disputes are resolved. When the "Chinese Model" is transplanted to another jurisdiction, the general legal and cultural background in that place deserves particular attention. As has been pointed out by Professor Chase, "[a]ny proposal to borrow procedures from another society should prompt a cultural inquiry."[85] If the jurisdiction does not have a settlement-preferred environment, or adjudication plays

[83] Kaufmann-Kohler and Kun 2008, p. 492.

[84] Chan 1997, p. 540.

[85] Chase 2005, p. 48. Specifically, Chase pointed out two questions that need to be born in mind: first, how will the borrowed approach work in a new social setting? Second, how will the introduced procedures impact the society that adopts them?

a dominant role in dispute resolution in its legal tradition, it could be hard to establish a dispute resolution system similar to that of China. Even if such a system is built, its practical effect would probably be limited. Thus, it is important to search for a culture-specific path, rather than simply transplanting elements from the "Chinese Model". In addition, considering the legal system is an inseparable whole, possible conflicts between the imported practice and the existing part of the home state's legal system are also necessary to be born in mind.

5.5 Conclusion

For FDI-related dispute resolution, China has built a system constituting of negotiation, mediation, arbitration, complaints coordination for foreign investment, administrative review and litigation. It is noticeable that amicable DSMs, especially mediation, are encouraged, and the whole system shows a tune of preferring amicable settlement. Such a practice is built on the basis of Chinese ideology where harmony is seen as the utmost task of the society and the core value of the design of DSMs. This ideology has its deep root in traditional Chinese philosophies, which have exerted and are expected to continue having great influence on the dispute resolution system in China.

The success of this "Chinese Model" will unavoidably affect other jurisdictions in the world to a certain extent, by promoting the status of amicable and informal DSMs for FDI-related disputes in domestic legal systems; at least, it provides a chance to the rest of the world to rethink the design of their dispute resolution systems. However, the real function of such Chinese experience in another jurisdiction will depend on how it is incorporated into a foreign legal environment, which includes the existing DSMs and the ideology of that society.

References

Bodde D, Morris C (1967) Law in imperial China. Harvard University Press, Cambridge, MA

Chan E (1997) Amicable Dispute Resolution in the People's Republic of China and Its Implications for Foreign-related Construction Disputes. Construction Management and Economics 15:543

Chase O (2005) Law, Culture, and Ritual—Disputing Systems in Cross-Cultural Context. New York University Press, New York/London

Fang T (2006) Negotiation: The Chinese style. Journal of Business & Industrial Marketing 21:55

Farina J (1989) "Talking Disputes into Harmony": China Approaches International Commercial Arbitration. American University International Law Review 4:157

Kaufmann-Kohler G, Kun F (2008) Integrating Mediation into Arbitration: Why It Works in China. Journal of International Arbitration 25:485

George H (1980) China, Modernization, and Sino-United States Trade: Will China Submit to Arbitration? California Western International Law Journal 10:68

Hu J (2003) Administrative Procedure Law Science. Higher Education Press, Beijing

Low P (1996) The Influence of Chinese Philosophies on Mediation and Conciliation in the Far East. Arbitration 62:3

Meski W (2009) Comparative Law in a Global Context: The Legal Systems of Asia and Africa. Cambridge University Press, Cambridge

Pan J (2011) Chinese Philosophy and International Law. Asian Journal of International Law 1:237

Scott D (1995) Seeking Harmony: Is the Asian Concept of the Conciliator/Arbitrator Applicable in the West? Dispute Resolution Journal 50:74

Sussman E (2009) Developing an Effective Med-Arb/Arb-Med Process. New York Dispute Resolution Lawyer 2:71–74

United Nations Conference on Trade and Development (UNCTAD) (2016) World Investment Report 2016. http://unctad.org/en/PublicationsLibrary/wir2016_en.pdf. Accessed 11 June 2017

United Nations Conference on Trade and Development (UNCTAD) (2015) World Investment Report 2015. http://unctad.org/en/PublicationsLibrary/wir2015_en.pdf. Accessed 11 June 2017

Wang G (2011) Chinese Mechanisms for Resolving Investor-State Disputes. Jindal Journal of International Affairs 1:211, 222

Wang S (2001) The Theory and Practice of Combining Arbitration with Conciliation. Publishing House of Law, Beijing

Wang Z (2012) Beijing Industry and Commerce Bureau Xicheng branch: Connecting Administrative Mediation of Contract Dispute Judicial Confirmation. http://news.hexun.com/2012-10-29/147305499.html. Accessed 11 June 2017

Zhang M (2010) The Socialist Legal System with Chinese Characteristics: China's Discourse for the Rule of Law and a Bitter Experience. Temple International & Comparative Law Journal 24:42

FSC
www.fsc.org
MIX
Papier | Fördert
gute Waldnutzung
FSC® C083411

Kolibri 360 GmbH
Ferdinand-Jühlke-Straße 7
99095 Erfurt, Deutschland
produktsicherheit@kolibri360.de